Copyright © 2022 by John Stahl

EMOJIs and the Roman Road #EmojiBibleProject by John Stahl

Email: EmojiGospel@gmail.com
Like us on Facebook: #EmojiBibleProject
Follow us on Twitter: @JustJesusThem
Website: www.PocketFullOfFaith.com

Printed in the United States of America
Edited by Rita Krajick, Khrystal Khoury, and Deanna Stahl

ISBN paperback 979-8-9870580-0-8

Published in Ohio by Pocket Full of Faith Productions in conjunction with Just Jesus Them Ministries.

www.PocketFullOfFaith.com

Cover Design by: George Dey
www.slimansprintery.com

Interior Design by: George Dey
www.slimansprintery.com

EMOJIs used in license agreement with JoyPixels.com.

Other #EmojiBibleProject Books
(Available at PocketFullOfFaith.com)

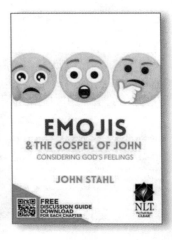

**FOR FREE DISCUSSION GUIDES/BIBLE STUDIES
GO TO THIS WEB ADDRESS:**

PocketFullOfFaith.com

— or —
Scan the QR Code Below:

SPECIAL THANKS:

To Kaitlyn and Johnny Yurkschatt, Bobby and Peggy Richards, Hernan and Tonya Restrepo, Keith and Lynette Collett, Rick and Mary Kay Stanley, Don Rine, Eric and Mary Ayer, Lisa, Dallas, John and Janelle Rasnick, Ben and Lorie Adams, Jim and Lisa Saxer, Ernie, Patty, Akron City Church, Gary and Melody Alto, Ryan and Nicole Burke, Ryan and Allison McGraw, Joanie and Steve Gulbronson, Rich and Karrie, CFC Largo, Nancy and Tony Antulis, Rob and Nelly Antulis, Jack and Charlene Chandler, David and Michelle Antulis, Paul and Teresa Stephens, Joe and Doreen Orlando, Tommy, Ty, Stefan, HighPoint Christian Church, the board of the #EmojiBibleProject: Zac, Ryan, and Jon, Connect Church, and all those that have supported me along the path of ministry over the years. May you always be doers of the Word. Hearing only makes us complacent and lazy. Be the Word and do the Word!

To George and Judi who believed in this project and were so kind in their effort and support! To Jeremy for stepping in and handling all kinds of things at just the right time. To John Morr for getting this off the ground with his technical skills.

To Rita Krajick, Khrystal, and Deanna for editing...ok, fixing all the grammatical issues.

To the folks at Tyndale Publishers House, Jessie, David, George, and the New Living Translation board, thank you for your support as we use such a recognizable and easy to read translation. It is up to us to study and share and teach God's word with others, but also to live it before them.

I pray this book helps do just that.

Learn It. Live It. Love others with It. What is "It"? The good news that God loves each of us so much that He sent His son Jesus so that we may live life to the fullest, both now and eternally.

4

Starting with the "Why?"

This book is not intended to replace the Bible. Nothing can do that. This is one piece of the Bible and is intended to help generations of all ages come together through the combination of God's Word and something that we all understand, use, and see almost every day: EMOJIs. Let's talk about the greatest story ever told and let's do so with someone we love!

The intention is to take one piece of the Bible and help people understand it and share it with others. It is also meant to study together and talk about the Word, the EMOJI tied to the Word, and, eventually, send us into the Bible to understand more of it.

We started with the Gospel of John and continued with the Missionary Journeys of Paul. The next step in the #EmojiBibleProject leads us to James, Peter, John, Jude and introduces us to the Old Testament starting with Ruth and Jonah.

As you read, may you consider the feelings of others. May you consider the writer, the reader, the people listening to each of the letters, and, most of all, God.

Lastly, the study notes may not be perfect. We did our best. But, God's Word is, and the impact those words have on each of us, ultimately, are what count.

James 1:22.
John 10:10.

The EMOJIS:

The Emotion Behind the EMOJIS:

 = Astonished or shocked

 = Think about it

 = Sadness

 = Thumbs up

 = Angel

 = Relieved

 = Angry

 = Numbers

 = The Cross

THE ROMAN ROAD

Why would God send his one and only son to die for the whole world? Why would God send his one only son to die for just you and me? After all, we are part of the world that he so loved that he gave Jesus to us.

John 3:16 says it best: *"For this is how God loved the world: He gave his one and only Son, so that everyone who believes in him will not perish but have eternal life.* This tells us "why" Jesus was sent for each of us.

But *how* do we get to Heaven where Jesus now is? That is what the Roman Road shares. It is the path to heaven for anyone who believes. In this book, it is marked easily, using the EMOJI for the cross:

If you are a person who has never taken the step of faith to God, you can go verse by verse using this cross to get to Jesus who not only died on the cross , but came back from the dead three days later. Jesus's coming back shows us there is hope. It showed us how much he loves us. And, it showed us that we can live life now through our faith in Jesus, with the promise of life with him forever.

The Roman Road Verses:

(You can turn to these verses at any time, including now, to follow the path to being saved. You can also turn to these verses at any time to share these verses with someone who also wants to know for sure they have a place in Heaven with a God who loves them so much that he gave everything for them.)

✝ Romans 3:23

✝ Romans 5:8

✝ Romans 6:23

✝ Romans 8:1

✝ Romans 10:8-13

Other verses from the Bible:

John 3:16-17 (😕 😮 😌 from EMOJIs and the Gospel of John)

Ephesians 2:8-9 (😌 😕 from EMOJIs and the Missionary Journeys of Paul)

Introduction to Romans - Chapter 1

Paul was originally known as Saul. He was a Pharisee. The Pharisees were a group of people that made all the rules and told people how they should live according to God's book of the law, the Torah (for more information on the Torah, see the introduction to Chapter 7 👍). The rules they made had nothing to do with Jesus.

At one time in his life, Paul hated Christians. He hated them so much that he wanted to kill them. One day, though, on a trip to seek out and kill Christians, he had an encounter with Jesus. At first, Paul lost his eyesight. Eventually, he got it back and eventually became the greatest missionary in the Bible. In fact, Paul became the greatest missionary ever. He planted churches all over the Roman Empire outside of Jerusalem. 😌

In this first chapter in the book of Romans, Paul talks about the Gentiles. If you aren't a Jew, meaning a person from Jerusalem, then you are a Gentile. Those are the two kinds of people you will find both in the Bible and in this world. Both the Jews and the Gentiles have missed the mark with God, which is the meaning of the word "sin". 😲

Romans 1:1 When he became a believer, Paul changed his name from Saul to Paul. Saul is a Hebrew name. Paul is a Roman name. Nowhere in the Bible does it tell us why he changed his name. But, based on his background and what he was taught, it gave Paul access to different areas in the Roman Empire, including Rome.

Romans 1:1 An apostle means "one who was sent". In other words, they were there to deliver a message. We start off as disciples (meaning "student"), just as the 12 disciples did with Jesus. Eventually, we go and share the message with other people in our world. That is the transition from disciple to apostle that we all must make in our walk of faith.

Romans Chapter One

Greetings from Paul

¹This letter is from Paul , a slave of Christ Jesus, chosen by God to be an apostle and sent out to preach his Good News. ² God promised this Good News long ago through his prophets in the holy Scriptures. ³ The Good News is about his Son. In his earthly life he was born into King David's family line, ⁴ and he was shown to be the Son of God when he was raised from the dead by the power of the Holy Spirit. He is Jesus Christ our Lord. ⁵ Through Christ, God has given us the privilege and authority as apostles to tell Gentiles everywhere what God has done for them, so that they will believe and obey him, bringing glory to his name.

⁶ And you are included among those Gentiles who have been called to belong to Jesus Christ. ⁷ I am writing to all of you in Rome who are loved by God and are called to be his own holy people.

May God our Father and the Lord Jesus Christ give you grace and peace.

God's Good News

[8] Let me say first that I thank my God through Jesus Christ for all of you, because your faith in him is being talked about all over the world. [9] God knows how often I pray for you. Day and night I bring you and your needs in prayer to God, whom I serve with all my heart by spreading the Good News about his Son.

[10] One of the things I always pray for is the opportunity, God willing, to come at last to see you. [11] For I long to visit you so I can bring you some spiritual gift that will help you grow strong in the Lord. [12] When we get together, I want to encourage you in your faith, but I also want to be encouraged by yours.

[13] I want you to know, dear brothers and sisters, that I planned many times to visit you, but I was prevented until now.

Romans 1:9 The Bible tells us in 1 Thessalonians 5:17 that we should pray without ceasing. This verse is the example of what that means. When we are serving God with all our heart, we can't help but talk to him throughout the day. So regardless of the time, day or night, when we see a need we talk to God about it.

Romans 1:12 This is why it is so important for us to meet as believers. It could be Sunday at church, a mid-week Bible study, youth group, camps, conferences, etc. We come together to lift others up when it comes to their faith, but we are also encouraged when we see people that live out their faith around us!

Romans 1:13

Galatians 5:22-23 tells us that the Holy Spirit produces the fruit Paul talks about here. That fruit is: love, joy, peace, patience, kindness, goodness, faithfulness, gentleness, and self-control.

Romans 1:16-19

We may not think that God feels anger, but these verses show us he does. What makes him angry? When people know the truth but try to take people away from that truth. What is the truth? According to verses 16 and 17, it is that God wants to save everyone – regardless of age, gender, race, or religion – by making us right in God's eyes.

I want to work among you and see spiritual fruit, just as I have seen among other Gentiles. [14] For I have a great sense of obligation to people in both the civilized world and the rest of the world, to the educated and uneducated alike. [15] So I am eager to come to you in Rome, too, to preach the Good News.

[16] For I am not ashamed of this Good News about Christ. It is the power of God at work, saving everyone who believes—the Jew first and also the Gentile. [17] This Good News tells us how God makes us right in his sight. This is accomplished from start to finish by faith. As the Scriptures say, "It is through faith that a righteous person has life."

God's Anger at Sin

[18] But God shows his anger from heaven against all sinful, wicked people who suppress the truth by their wickedness. [19] They know the truth about God because he has made it obvious to them.

[20] For ever since the world was created, people have seen the earth and sky. Through everything God made, they can clearly see his invisible qualities—his eternal power and divine nature. So they have no excuse for not knowing God.

[21] Yes, they knew God, but they wouldn't worship him as God or even give him thanks. And they began to think up foolish ideas of what God was like. As a result, their minds became dark and confused. [22] Claiming to be wise, they instead became utter fools. [23] And instead of worshiping the glorious, ever-living God, they worshiped idols made to look like mere people and birds and animals and reptiles.

[24] So God abandoned them to do whatever shameful things their hearts desired. As a result, they did vile and degrading things with each other's bodies. [25] They traded the truth about God for a lie. So they worshiped and served the things God created instead of the Creator himself, who is worthy of eternal praise! Amen.

Romans 1:20 Paul shares with us that we have no excuse for not knowing God. Here are great examples of how easy it is for us to miss God:
A person whispered, "God, speak to me." And a bird sang. But this person did not hear. So, the person yelled, "God, speak to me!" Thunder rolled across the sky. But they did not listen. The person looked around and said, "God, let me see you." A star shone brightly. But they did not notice it. And the person shouted, "God, show me a miracle." And a life was born. But they were unaware. So, this person cried out in despair, "Touch me, God, and let me know that you are here!" Then God reached down and touched this person. But the person brushed the butterfly away and walked on, left searching for God who was already there. (Author unknown)

Romans 1:29-31 If you have ever wanted a list of what to avoid when it comes to missing the mark with God, these verses give that to us.

26 That is why God abandoned them to their shameful desires. Even the women turned against the natural way to have sex and instead indulged in sex with each other. 27 And the men, instead of having normal sexual relations with women, burned with lust for each other. Men did shameful things with other men, and as a result of this sin, they suffered within themselves the penalty they deserved.

28 Since they thought it foolish to acknowledge God, he abandoned them to their foolish thinking and let them do things that should never be done. 29 Their lives became full of every kind of wickedness, sin, greed, hate, envy, murder, quarreling, deception, malicious behavior, and gossip. 30 They are backstabbers, haters of God, insolent, proud, and boastful. They invent new ways of sinning, and they disobey their parents. 31 They refuse to understand, break their promises, are heartless, and have no mercy.

[32] They know God's justice requires that those who do these things deserve to die, yet they do them anyway. Worse yet, they encourage others to do them, too.

Introduction to Romans - Chapter 2

In chapter two, Paul shifts his focus back to the Jewish people. Remember, these are his people, and he is one of them. They, too, have missed the mark, and have lost sight of God.

The Jews, like the Gentiles, like us today, have been beat up so badly by the world, and are tired and broken. They are all in need of something, and, as Paul will show them, that something is Jesus. Jesus didn't come to put them down, make fun of them, and show them every command they had broken. No, God had sent his one and only son because they needed a savior. Jesus came to save each of them and all of them, both Jew and Gentile. And that includes us!

Romans 2:1-3 Many people believe that John 3:16 is the most quoted verse in the Bible. Sadly, that is not true. The most quoted verse in the Bible is Matthew 7:1 "Do not judge or you, too, will be judged." Paul expands on that in these verses as he shares how easy it is for us to judge others and choose not to look at ourselves personally first. Our job isn't to judge others. Our job is to weigh our words, thoughts, and actions according to what God's Word teaches us. A word of caution: that doesn't mean we shouldn't use our best judgment when it comes to situations that appear wrong. God gives us the gift of discernment to seek him for guidance in areas that don't seem right to us.

Romans Chapter Two

God's Judgment of Sin

¹You may think you can condemn such people, but you are just as bad, and you have no excuse! When you say they are wicked and should be punished, you are condemning yourself, for you who judge others do these very same things. ²And we know that God, in his justice, will punish anyone who does such things. ³Since you judge others for doing these things, why do you think you can avoid God's judgment when you do the same things? ⁴Don't you see how wonderfully kind, tolerant, and patient God is with you? Does this mean nothing to you? Can't you see that his kindness is intended to turn you from your sin?

⁵But because you are stubborn and refuse to turn from your sin, you are storing up terrible punishment for yourself. For a day of anger is coming, when God's righteous judgment will be revealed. ⁶He will judge everyone according to what they have done.

⁷ He will give eternal life to those who keep on doing good, seeking after the glory and honor and immortality that God offers.

⁸ But he will pour out his anger and wrath on those who live for themselves, who refuse to obey the truth and instead live lives of wickedness. ⁹ There will be trouble and calamity for everyone who keeps on doing what is evil—for the Jew first and also for the Gentile. ¹⁰ But there will be glory and honor and peace from God for all who do good—for the Jew first and also for the Gentile. ¹¹ For God does not show favoritism.

¹² When the Gentiles sin, they will be destroyed, even though they never had God's written law. And the Jews, who do have God's law, will be judged by that law when they fail to obey it. ¹³ For merely listening to the law doesn't make us right with God. It is obeying the law that makes us right in his sight.

Romans 2:7 This verse doesn't mean that the good we do can get us to heaven. It means that the good we do points to what God has done for us in this life, which leads to eternal life. Because we are thankful and grateful, our lives show it in the words and actions we use around others. It isn't faith or works. It isn't faith and works. It is faith *that* works.

Romans 2:14 There are two kinds of people in the Bible. The Jews and the Gentiles. A Gentile is anyone that isn't a Jew, which is most of us both then and now.

Romans 2:14-15 Almost everyone knows right from wrong, and many times choose to do the right thing because it is the right thing to do – even if they don't know God personally. God invites us in, though, so that we can look, learn, and live by faith which can help us now and for eternity. There is never a wrong time to do the right thing but doing the right thing because God has put that on our heart changes us from the inside out.

14 Even Gentiles, who do not have God's written law, show that they know his law when they instinctively obey it, even without having heard it. 15 They demonstrate that God's law is written in their hearts, for their own conscience and thoughts either accuse them or tell them they are doing right. 16 And this is the message I proclaim—that the day is coming when God, through Christ Jesus, will judge everyone's secret life.

The Jews and the Law

17 You who call yourselves Jews are relying on God's law, and you boast about your special relationship with him. 18 You know what he wants; you know what is right because you have been taught his law. 19 You are convinced that you are a guide for the blind and a light for people who are lost in darkness. 20 You think you can instruct the ignorant and teach children the ways of God. For you are certain that God's law gives you complete knowledge and truth.

[21] Well then, if you teach others, why don't you teach yourself? You tell others not to steal, but do you steal? [22] You say it is wrong to commit adultery, but do you commit adultery? You condemn idolatry, but do you use items stolen from pagan temples? [23] You are so proud of knowing the law, but you dishonor God by breaking it. [24] No wonder the Scriptures say, "The Gentiles blaspheme the name of God because of you."

[25] The Jewish ceremony of circumcision has value only if you obey God's law. But if you don't obey God's law, you are no better off than an uncircumcised Gentile. [26] And if the Gentiles obey God's law, won't God declare them to be his own people? [27] In fact, uncircumcised Gentiles who keep God's law will condemn you Jews who are circumcised and possess God's law but don't obey it.

Romans 2:21-24

Alexander the Great was one of the most powerful rulers in history. A story goes that a young soldier was not doing his job and ran from the enemy. He came before this great ruler and was asked his name. When the young soldier said "Alexander", the great ruler became very angry. The mighty ruler grabbed the young soldier and threw him to the ground and gave him a choice: change your ways or change your name. As a believer we are called Christians. That means we are to be "mini-Christs". If we carry that name, the way that we act should reflect the kind, caring, and loving savior of Jesus Christ, who brought peace, hope, and love to those he served every day.

Romans 2:29 If you are a believer, would you say that you are more focused on seeking praise from God or people? In other words, are you a people pleaser or a God pleaser?

[28] For you are not a true Jew just because you were born of Jewish parents or because you have gone through the ceremony of circumcision. [29] No, a true Jew is one whose heart is right with God. And true circumcision is not merely obeying the letter of the law; rather, it is a change of heart produced by the Spirit. And a person with a changed heart seeks praise from God, not from people.

Introduction to Romans - Chapter 3

This chapter starts with Paul explaining that everyone has missed the mark with God. Everyone meaning both Jews and Gentiles. And missing the mark meaning sin.

This chapter introduces us to the start of the Roman road (verse 3:23). This is the path to salvation. Paul explains that Jesus was the sacrifice for all our sins. The sacrifice that Jesus made was for everyone. And for all who trust and believe in Him and that believe that Jesus made this sacrifice for them personally, they can accept Jesus as their savior and be saved. As Paul shares, Jesus is the very Messiah that the Jewish people have all been looking and waiting for all these years.

Romans Chapter Three

God Remains Faithful

¹Then what's the advantage of being a Jew? Is there any value in the ceremony of circumcision? ²Yes, there are great benefits! First of all, the Jews were entrusted with the whole revelation of God.

³True, some of them were unfaithful; but just because they were unfaithful, does that mean God will be unfaithful? ⁴Of course not! Even if everyone else is a liar, God is true. As the Scriptures say about him,

"You will be proved right in what you say,
and you will win your case in court."

⁵"But," some might say, "our sinfulness serves a good purpose, for it helps people see how righteous God is. Isn't it unfair, then, for him to punish us?" (This is merely a human point of view.)

⁶ Of course not! If God were not entirely fair, how would he be qualified to judge the world? ⁷ "But," someone might still argue, "how can God condemn me as a sinner if my dishonesty highlights his truthfulness and brings him more glory?" ⁸ And some people even slander us by claiming that we say, "The more we sin, the better it is!" Those who say such things deserve to be condemned.

All People Are Sinners

⁹ Well then, should we conclude that we Jews are better than others? No, not at all, for we have already shown that all people, whether Jews or Gentiles, are under the power of sin. ¹⁰ As the Scriptures say,

> "No one is righteous—
>   not even one.
> ¹¹ No one is truly wise;
> no one is seeking God.
> ¹² All have turned away;
> all have become useless.
> No one does good,
>
> not a single one."

Romans 3:10-12 We will share often that sin means "to miss the mark". This verse shows that each and every one of us miss the mark. When it comes to God, if you miss him by an inch or 100 kilometers or 100 miles, you still miss God. Remember, if you miss God by a second, a day, or 50 years, you can miss God for eternity.

👍 **Romans 3:10-18**

Notice that each of these verses start and end in quotation marks? That is because Paul is sharing words from the Old Testament. He is sharing the exact words from the book of law that the Jews who were listening or reading would be able to understand. In other words, Paul is quoting Scripture (the Bible) to teach them.

¹³ "Their talk is foul, like the stench from an open grave.

Their tongues are filled with lies." "Snake venom drips from their lips."

¹⁴ "Their mouths are full of cursing and bitterness."

¹⁵ "They rush to commit murder.

¹⁶ Destruction and misery always follow them.

¹⁷ They don't know where to find peace."

¹⁸ "They have no fear of God at all." 👍

¹⁹ Obviously, the law applies to those to whom it was given, for its purpose is to keep people from having excuses, and to show that the entire world is guilty before God. ²⁰ For no one can ever be made right with God by doing what the law commands. The law simply shows us how sinful we are.

Christ Took Our Punishment

²¹ But now God has shown us a way to be made right with him without keeping the requirements of the law, as was promised in the writings of Moses and the prophets long ago.

²² We are made right with God by placing our faith in Jesus Christ. And this is true for everyone who believes, no matter who we are.

²³ For everyone has sinned; we all fall short of God's glorious standard. ✝ ²⁴ Yet God, in his grace, freely makes us right in his sight. He did this through Christ Jesus when he freed us from the penalty for our sins. ²⁵ For God presented Jesus as the sacrifice for sin. People are made right with God when they believe that Jesus sacrificed his life, shedding his blood. This sacrifice shows that God was being fair when he held back and did not punish those who sinned in times past, ²⁶ for he was looking ahead and including them in what he would do in this present time. God did this to demonstrate his righteousness, for he himself is fair and just, and he makes sinners right in his sight when they believe in Jesus.

✝ **Romans 3:23** This is the start of the Roman Road. It is a path traveled to teach others about the gift of salvation. You can follow the road personally so you can know that you will have a place in heaven when you take a step of faith and ask Jesus into your heart as your personal savior. You can also share this with others so they, too, can know for sure that they can also have that same gift.

(Here are the verses you can follow, in order, in the book of Romans for the plan of salvation: Romans 3:23; Romans 5:8; Romans 6:23; Romans 8:1 Romans 10:8-13.)

Other verses that support these can be found in EMOJIs and the Gospel of John: John 3:16-17 and EMOJIs and the Missionary Journeys of Paul: Ephesians 2:8-9

Romans 3:29-31

The law (Old Testament) was given to the Jews so they knew how to live and treat each other, while also showing respect to God. The love (New Testament) was given to us through Jesus as a gift as God was showing us that he is a relational God. But God's love never canceled out God's law. They are both needed so we can treat others with the kind of respect in this world that can only show God's love!

²⁷ Can we boast, then, that we have done anything to be accepted by God? No, because our acquittal is not based on obeying the law. It is based on faith. ²⁸ So we are made right with God through faith and not by obeying the law.

²⁹ After all, is God the God of the Jews only? Isn't he also the God of the Gentiles? Of course he is. ³⁰ There is only one God, and he makes people right with himself only by faith, whether they are Jews or Gentiles. ³¹ Well then, if we emphasize faith, does this mean that we can forget about the law? Of course not! In fact, only when we have faith do we truly fulfill the law.

Introduction to Romans - Chapter 4

Paul shares from the Old Testament about Father Abraham. Father Abraham was literally the father of all nations as promised by God. The Old Testament idea was that God was there for everyone. Somewhere along the way this was lost.

Just as people trusted that God blessed Abraham as the father of all nations, it was now time to put their trust in Jesus, God's one and only son, as the Messiah and savior of the world. Remember, Jesus died on the cross but rose from the dead again three days later. This showed everyone that they could have eternal life when they trusted and believed in him.

Romans Chapter Four

The Faith of Abraham

¹ Abraham was, humanly speaking, the founder of our Jewish nation. What did he discover about being made right with God? ² If his good deeds had made him acceptable to God, he would have had something to boast about. But that was not God's way. ³ For the Scriptures tell us, "Abraham believed God, and God counted him as righteous because of his faith."

⁴ When people work, their wages are not a gift, but something they have earned. ⁵ But people are counted as righteous, not because of their work, but because of their faith in God who forgives sinners. ⁶ David also spoke of this when he described the happiness of those who are declared righteous without working for it:

⁷ "Oh, what joy for those
   whose disobedience is
      forgiven,
whose sins are put out of sight.

⁸ Yes, what joy for those whose record the LORD has cleared of sin." 😌

⁹ Now, is this blessing only for the Jews, or is it also for uncircumcised Gentiles? Well, we have been saying that Abraham was counted as righteous by God because of his faith. ¹⁰ But how did this happen? Was he counted as righteous only after he was circumcised, or was it before he was circumcised? Clearly, God accepted Abraham before he was circumcised!

¹¹ Circumcision was a sign that Abraham already had faith and that God had already accepted him and declared him to be righteous—even before he was circumcised. So Abraham is the spiritual father of those who have faith but have not been circumcised. They are counted as righteous because of their faith. ¹² And Abraham is also the spiritual father of those who have been circumcised, but only if they have the same kind of faith Abraham had before he was circumcised.

😌 **Romans 4:8** Paul is sharing a lesson from Psalm 32:1-2. It is so easy for us to focus on guilt when it comes to our relationship with God and others. That is why God sent Jesus for each of us. God doesn't want us to rest in guilt, he wants us to focus on grace. Paul also wrote that it is by grace - not guilt - that we are saved through our faith! (Ephesians 2:8-9).

👍 **Romans 4:13-14** In the study note for Romans 4:1-4 we shared that it isn't faith or works and it isn't faith and works, it is faith that works. This verse supports this further. If we follow the law and the commandments, our focus is on doing good. But, how much good will get us to heaven? That is why it isn't what we do that gets us to heaven, but rather what God has done. He sent his one and only son for each of us. This includes every person that ever came from Abraham, the father of all nations, who had the faith to trust and believe God's promise.

[13] Clearly, God's promise to give the whole earth to Abraham and his descendants was based not on his obedience to God's law, but on a right relationship with God that comes by faith. [14] If God's promise is only for those who obey the law, then faith is not necessary and the promise is pointless. 👍 [15] For the law always brings punishment on those who try to obey it. (The only way to avoid breaking the law is to have no law to break!)

[16] So the promise is received by faith. It is given as a free gift. And we are all certain to receive it, whether or not we live according to the law of Moses, if we have faith like Abraham's. For Abraham is the father of all who believe. [17] That is what the Scriptures mean when God told him, "I have made you the father of many nations." This happened because Abraham believed in the God who brings the dead back to life and who creates new things out of nothing.

[18] Even when there was no reason for hope, Abraham kept hoping—believing that he would become the father of many nations. For God had said to him, "That's how many descendants you will have!" [19] And Abraham's faith did not weaken, even though, at about 100 years of age, he figured his body was as good as dead—and so was Sarah's womb.

[20] Abraham never wavered in believing God's promise. In fact, his faith grew stronger, and in this he brought glory to God. [21] He was fully convinced that God is able to do whatever he promises. [22] And because of Abraham's faith, God counted him as righteous. [23] And when God counted him as righteous, it wasn't just for Abraham's benefit. It was recorded [24] for our benefit, too, assuring us that God will also count us as righteous if we believe in him, the one who raised Jesus our Lord from the dead. [25] He was handed over to die because of our sins, and he was raised to life to make us right with God.

Romans 4:19 This verse shows us God doesn't care about our age when it comes to our walk of faith. God can answer prayer at any time, regardless of how old or young we are. Abraham had to wait until he was 100 years old before he knew that he and his wife, Sarah, would have the baby they wanted their entire married life! (His name was Isaac and you can read about Isaac's story in Genesis, the first book of the Bible, in chapters 17, 21, 22, 24, 25, 26, 27, 28, 31, and 35.)

Introduction to Romans - Chapter 5

In this chapter, Paul shares that we all have a place in God's family. Paul starts by using someone that would be familiar to his audience. He talks about Adam, the first person ever made. He shares how sin entered the world through Adam and Eve and because of this, along came with it, death. He then brings up Jesus and how he carried the sin of the entire world to his death. By doing so and rising from the dead, Jesus brought us life that we could all have forever.

Paul also shares that for anyone that accepts this gift that their life will be different. They have changed from the inside out. They won't live as this world lives. Instead, they will live as God would want them to live.

Romans Chapter Five

Faith Brings Joy

¹Therefore, since we have been made right in God's sight by faith, we have peace with God because of what Jesus Christ our Lord has done for us. ²Because of our faith, Christ has brought us into this place of undeserved privilege where we now stand, and we confidently and joyfully look forward to sharing God's glory.

³ We can rejoice, too, when we run into problems and trials, for we know that they help us develop endurance. ⁴ And endurance develops strength of character, and character strengthens our confident hope of salvation. ⁵ And this hope will not lead to disappointment. For we know how dearly God loves us, because he has given us the Holy Spirit to fill our hearts with his love.

⁶ When we were utterly helpless, Christ came at just the right time and died for us sinners.

[7] Now, most people would not be willing to die for an upright person, though someone might perhaps be willing to die for a person who is especially good. [8] But God showed his great love for us by sending Christ to die for us while we were still sinners.

[9] And since we have been made right in God's sight by the blood of Christ, he will certainly save us from God's condemnation. [10] For since our friendship with God was restored by the death of his Son while we were still his enemies, we will certainly be saved through the life of his Son. [11] So now we can rejoice in our wonderful new relationship with God because our Lord Jesus Christ has made us friends of God.

Adam and Christ Contrasted

[12] When Adam sinned, sin entered the world. Adam's sin brought death, so death spread to everyone, for everyone sinned. [13] Yes, people sinned even before the law was given.

Romans 5:8 This is the second verse of the "Roman Road", which teaches us how to share salvation with someone that wants to know for sure they have a place in Heaven with a loving Heavenly Father. This verse shares with us that Jesus Christ died for our sins.

(Here are the verses you can follow, in order, in the book of Romans for the plan of salvation: Romans 3:23; Romans 5:8; Romans 6:23; Romans 8:1; Romans 10:8-13.)

Romans 5:7-11 The theme of this section is not only our salvation, but friendship. This is something we do not often think or even talk about, yet, when we have a right relationship with God, we are not only part of his family, but we are also God's friends.

But it was not counted as sin, because there was not yet any law to break. ¹⁴ Still, everyone died—from the time of Adam to the time of Moses—even those who did not disobey an explicit commandment of God, as Adam did. Now Adam is a symbol, a representation of Christ, who was yet to come. ¹⁵ But there is a great difference between Adam's sin and God's gracious gift. For the sin of this one man, Adam, brought death to many. But even greater is God's wonderful grace and his gift of forgiveness to many through this other man, Jesus Christ. ¹⁶ And the result of God's gracious gift is very different from the result of that one man's sin. For Adam's sin led to condemnation, but God's free gift leads to our being made right with God, even though we are guilty of many sins. ¹⁷ For the sin of this one man, Adam, caused death to rule over many. But even greater is God's wonderful grace and his gift of righteousness, for all who receive it will live in triumph over sin and death through this one man, Jesus Christ.

¹⁸ Yes, Adam's one sin brings condemnation for everyone, but Christ's one act of righteousness brings a right relationship with God and new life for everyone.

¹⁹ Because one person disobeyed God, many became sinners. But because one other person obeyed God, many will be made righteous.

²⁰ God's law was given so that all people could see how sinful they were. But as people sinned more and more, God's wonderful grace became more abundant. ²¹ So just as sin ruled over all people and brought them to death, now God's wonderful grace rules instead, giving us right standing with God and resulting in eternal life through Jesus Christ our Lord.

Romans 5:18 this seems like a difficult concept to grasp but it doesn't have to be. Simply put, if we focus on just the Old Testament and the law, we die with this as there is no hope. Through the New Testament with Jesus Christ, the old is washed away and we have a new, eternal life as we now have a right relationship with God!

Introduction to Romans - Chapter 6

In this chapter Paul uses baptism as a symbol. when we choose baptism, we are going public with our faith. 👍 When we are taken down into the water it is the same as when Jesus died on the cross. It is a symbol of us dying to our sin. When we are raised out of the water everything starts brand new. Because of this, our lives should reflect that newfound faith and life. 😷

Remember that as followers of Jesus that means we are called Christians. Christians literally means "mini-Christs". This means that we should live in such a way that people can't help but see Jesus through us. 😌

Romans 6:1-4

Baptism is something that is different in every church. Some sprinkle the person being baptized. Some completely immerse the person being baptized one time. Still others immerse the person multiple times. Baptism at this time was by immersion, as the example was John the Baptist using the Jordan river for baptisms (including baptizing Jesus – see Matthew 3:11-17, Mark 1:7-11 or Luke 3:21-22 to read about this event). Going into the water was dying to yourself (as Jesus did on the cross) and coming out of the water meant new life to the believer (as Jesus did when he rose from the dead).

Sin's Power Is Broken

¹ Well then, should we keep on sinning so that God can show us more and more of his wonderful grace? ² Of course not! Since we have died to sin, how can we continue to live in it? ³ Or have you forgotten that when we were joined with Christ Jesus in baptism, we joined him in his death? ⁴ For we died and were buried with Christ by baptism. And just as Christ was raised from the dead by the glorious power of the Father, now we also may live new lives.

⁵ Since we have been united with him in his death, we will also be raised to life as he was. ⁶ We know that our old sinful selves were crucified with Christ so that sin might lose its power in our lives. We are no longer slaves to sin. ⁷ For when we died with Christ we were set free from the power of sin.

⁸ And since we died with Christ, we know we will also live with him. ⁹ We are sure of this because Christ was raised from the dead, and he will never die again. Death no longer has any power over him.

¹⁰ When he died, he died once to break the power of sin. But now that he lives, he lives for the glory of God. ¹¹ So you also should consider yourselves to be dead to the power of sin and alive to God through Christ Jesus.

¹² Do not let sin control the way you live; do not give in to sinful desires. ¹³ Do not let any part of your body become an instrument of evil to serve sin. Instead, give yourselves completely to God, for you were dead, but now you have new life. So use your whole body as an instrument to do what is right for the glory of God. ¹⁴ Sin is no longer your master, for you no longer live under the requirements of the law. Instead, you live under the freedom of God's grace.

Romans 6:10-11
When Jesus died on the cross, he broke the power of sin for the entire world. When Jesus came back from the dead, he proved the power was broken and that life comes from God. Jesus not only broke the power of sin, but he also took on the penalty of the sin through his death. Still, there was life through Jesus after death, which is offered to each of us. If we die to our sin, we live through God and his power.

Romans 6:15-16
There are people that believe in God, but do not follow God. The choices they make in life prove this. The way we live our life is either going to show others a loving God or show others that what we care about the most is ourselves and this world.

[15] Well then, since God's grace has set us free from the law, does that mean we can go on sinning? Of course not! [16] Don't you realize that you become the slave of whatever you choose to obey? You can be a slave to sin, which leads to death, or you can choose to obey God, which leads to righteous living.

[17] Thank God! Once you were slaves of sin, but now you wholeheartedly obey this teaching we have given you. [18] Now you are free from your slavery to sin, and you have become slaves to righteous living.

[19] Because of the weakness of your human nature, I am using the illustration of slavery to help you understand all this. Previously, you let yourselves be slaves to impurity and lawlessness, which led ever deeper into sin. Now you must give yourselves to be slaves to righteous living so that you will become holy.

[20] When you were slaves to sin, you were free from the obligation to do right. [21] And what was the result? You are now ashamed of the things you used to do, things that end in eternal doom. [22] But now you are free from the power of sin and have become slaves of God. Now you do those things that lead to holiness and result in eternal life. [23] For the wages of sin is death, but the free gift of God is eternal life through Christ Jesus our Lord.

Romans 6:23 This is the third verse of the "Roman Road", which teaches us how to share salvation with someone that wants to know for sure they have a place in Heaven with a loving Heavenly Father.

Each of us gets to choose where we spend eternity. If we choose to sin - meaning miss the mark – against God, we choose to walk as this world does and not in faith. God is a gentleman, though, and is not going to force himself on any of us. God does offer us a way to Him forever by giving us the gift of eternal life. Romans 6:23 tells us that this gift comes from God through his son, Jesus. The offer is to each of us, but it is our choice personally to accept this gift through our faith.

(Here are the verses you can follow, in order, in the book of Romans for the plan of salvation: Romans 3:23; Romans 5:8; Romans 6:23; Romans 8:1; Romans 10:8-13.)

Introduction to Romans - Chapter 7

Paul focuses on the law in this chapter. The law can be looked at in a couple different ways. The first way is what is known as the Pentateuch. These are the first five books of the Bible which were written by Moses. ⊞ They are also known as the Torah. The second way is through the commandments.

Many of us know that God gave us the 10 commandments through Moses on Mount Sinai. What most people don't know is that there are over 600 commandments in the Old Testament. ⊞

Romans 7:4 This is a verse that brings us hope in our everyday life. It is so positive and encouraging. We can all do good deeds for others. When a farmer brings in a harvest, he not only shows the crop that he grew, but he shares it with others. This is the same for us when we harvest good deeds for God.

No Longer Bound to the Law

[1] Now, dear brothers and sisters— you who are familiar with the law— don't you know that the law applies only while a person is living? [2] For example, when a woman marries, the law binds her to her husband as long as he is alive. But if he dies, the laws of marriage no longer apply to her. [3] So while her husband is alive, she would be committing adultery if she married another man. But if her husband dies, she is free from that law and does not commit adultery when she remarries.

[4] So, my dear brothers and sisters, this is the point: You died to the power of the law when you died with Christ. And now you are united with the one who was raised from the dead. As a result, we can produce a harvest of good deeds for God.

⁵ When we were controlled by our old nature, sinful desires were at work within us, and the law aroused these evil desires that produced a harvest of sinful deeds, resulting in death. ⁶ But now we have been released from the law, for we died to it and are no longer captive to its power. Now we can serve God, not in the old way of obeying the letter of the law, but in the new way of living in the Spirit.

Romans 7:6 Here is the beauty of accepting Jesus as your savior. We break the bonds of living in every rule and trying to keep every commandment and get to live, serve, and care for others in love by walking in the spirit Jesus promised us: the Holy Spirit.

God's Law Reveals Our Sin

⁷ Well then, am I suggesting that the law of God is sinful? Of course not! In fact, it was the law that showed me my sin. I would never have known that coveting is wrong if the law had not said, "You must not covet." ⁸ But sin used this command to arouse all kinds of covetous desires within me! If there were no law, sin would not have that power.

Romans 7:9-12

Depending on the version of the Bible that you read there are anywhere from 600 to 630 different commands from the Old Testament. What Paul is trying to share here is that it is so difficult to keep all of those. the commands were meant to guide us in our everyday life. The problem was that Paul, and others, were so focused on keeping the different commandments that they lost sight of God. Whenever we, just like Paul, lose sight of God we become spiritually dead.

⁹ At one time I lived without understanding the law. But when I learned the command not to covet, for instance, the power of sin came to life, ¹⁰ and I died. So I discovered that the law's commands, which were supposed to bring life, brought spiritual death instead. ¹¹ Sin took advantage of those commands and deceived me; it used the commands to kill me. ¹² But still, the law itself is holy, and its commands are holy and right and good.

¹³ But how can that be? Did the law, which is good, cause my death? Of course not! Sin used what was good to bring about my condemnation to death. So we can see how terrible sin really is. It uses God's good commands for its own evil purposes.

Struggling with Sin

¹⁴ So the trouble is not with the law, for it is spiritual and good. The trouble is with me, for I am all too human, a slave to sin.

[15] I don't really understand myself, for I want to do what is right, but I don't do it. Instead, I do what I hate. [16] But if I know that what I am doing is wrong, this shows that I agree that the law is good. [17] So I am not the one doing wrong; it is sin living in me that does it.

[18] And I know that nothing good lives in me, that is, in my sinful nature. I want to do what is right, but I can't. [19] I want to do what is good, but I don't. I don't want to do what is wrong, but I do it anyway. [20] But if I do what I don't want to do, I am not really the one doing wrong; it is sin living in me that does it.

[21] I have discovered this principle of life—that when I want to do what is right, I inevitably do what is wrong. [22] I love God's law with all my heart. [23] But there is another power within me that is at war with my mind. This power makes me a slave to the sin that is still within me.

Romans 7:15-20
This is a time where Paul is looking at himself and the things he does. This can be in the words he speaks, how he treats others, or even his thoughts. Paul admits here that he is a sinner and struggles with sin. We all struggle with sin (see Romans 3:23 and you will see that we are all sinners). All of us want to do the right thing, yet we somehow struggle with this every day. Paul is being honest with himself and his readers in these verses but is also letting them know they are not alone, just as you and I are not alone in our struggles.

Romans 7:24-25

Sadly, we all miss the mark with God at times. This can be in the words we use or our actions. We all have things we need to work on and give to God. Too many times, though, we just keep on missing the mark - sinning – because it is part of who we are. This is another reason we need God every day.

²⁴ Oh, what a miserable person I am! Who will free me from this life that is dominated by sin and death? ²⁵ Thank God! The answer is in Jesus Christ our Lord. So you see how it is: In my mind I really want to obey God's law, but because of my sinful nature I am a slave to sin.

Introduction to Romans - Chapter 8

Paul shifts from the law to love in chapter eight. There are so many commandments for people to keep that they just couldn't do so. In the end, people just felt guilty about it. God solved this by sending his son Jesus. This didn't put away the law. It just allowed people to focus on the love that God has for us.

There was more to Jesus than just living on this earth, as well. When he left, he promised us the Holy Spirit. It is through this spirit that we can seek counsel and comfort. When Jesus paid the ultimate sacrifice on the cross he did so for every single person in this world. And after he rose from the dead and went back to Heaven, he left his spirit for all who believe.

Romans Chapter Eight

Life in the Spirit

[1] So now there is no condemnation for those who belong to Christ Jesus. [2] And because you belong to him, the power of the life-giving Spirit has freed you from the power of sin that leads to death. [3] The law of Moses was unable to save us because of the weakness of our sinful nature. So God did what the law could not do. He sent his own Son in a body like the bodies we sinners have. And in that body God declared an end to sin's control over us by giving his Son as a sacrifice for our sins. [4] He did this so that the just requirement of the law would be fully satisfied for us, who no longer follow our sinful nature but instead follow the Spirit.

[5] Those who are dominated by the sinful nature think about sinful things, but those who are controlled by the Holy Spirit think about things that please the Spirit.

6 So letting your sinful nature control your mind leads to death. But letting the Spirit control your mind leads to life and peace.

7 For the sinful nature is always hostile to God. It never did obey God's laws, and it never will. 8 That's why those who are still under the control of their sinful nature can never please God.

9 But you are not controlled by your sinful nature. You are controlled by the Spirit if you have the Spirit of God living in you. (And remember that those who do not have the Spirit of Christ living in them do not belong to him at all.) 10 And Christ lives within you, so even though your body will die because of sin, the Spirit gives you life because you have been made right with God. 11 The Spirit of God, who raised Jesus from the dead, lives in you. And just as God raised Christ Jesus from the dead, he will give life to your mortal bodies by this same Spirit living within you.

Romans 8:6 this is such a great promise that we have from God. It is one of those simple sentences that we often overlook but there is hope in this that we can carry with us every day. When we allow God's Holy Spirit to control our mind it leads us to this: both life and peace. As a believer those are two gifts we can celebrate from God.

Romans 8:12-14

Whenever we see the word "therefore" we should stop and ask ourselves "what is that there for?" The word is always followed with the answer. In this verse, we don't have to give in to the little voice inside that is telling us to do something that we know God would not want us to do. Instead, God gives us the Holy Spirit that we can also listen for and follow to do the things that God would want us to do.

[12] Therefore, dear brothers and sisters, you have no obligation to do what your sinful nature urges you to do. [13] For if you live by its dictates, you will die. But if through the power of the Spirit you put to death the deeds of your sinful nature, you will live. [14] For all who are led by the Spirit of God are children of God.

[15] So you have not received a spirit that makes you fearful slaves. Instead, you received God's Spirit when he adopted you as his own children. Now we call him, "Abba, Father." [16] For his Spirit joins with our spirit to affirm that we are God's children. [17] And since we are his children, we are his heirs. In fact, together with Christ we are heirs of God's glory. But if we are to share his glory, we must also share his suffering.

The Future Glory

[18] Yet what we suffer now is nothing compared to the glory he will reveal to us later.

¹⁹ For all creation is waiting eagerly for that future day when God will reveal who his children really are. ²⁰ Against its will, all creation was subjected to God's curse. But with eager hope, ²¹ the creation looks forward to the day when it will join God's children in glorious freedom from death and decay. ²² For we know that all creation has been groaning as in the pains of childbirth right up to the present time. ²³ And we believers also groan, even though we have the Holy Spirit within us as a foretaste of future glory, for we long for our bodies to be released from sin and suffering. We, too, wait with eager hope for the day when God will give us our full rights as his adopted children, including the new bodies he has promised us. ²⁴ We were given this hope when we were saved. (If we already have something, we don't need to hope for it. ²⁵ But if we look forward to something we don't yet have, we must wait patiently and confidently.)

Romans 8:19-25 The "creation" is the world and everything in it. That means you and I are part of the creation. The "Creator" is God. God made the creation. As part of God's creation, what we worship is a personal choice. As you read these verses, ask yourself this question: am I more focused on the creation, or the Creator?

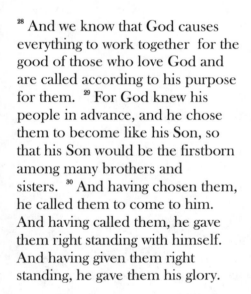

Romans 8:26-27

Have you ever thought about the Holy Spirit praying for you? God loves us so much that he sent his one and only son for us. Jesus loves us so much that he left his Holy Spirit for us. The Holy Spirit loves us so much that he prays for us. God the Father, God the Son, and God the Holy Spirit are in harmony with one another, and want us to be in harmony with them to match the will of God.

²⁶ And the Holy Spirit helps us in our weakness. For example, we don't know what God wants us to pray for. But the Holy Spirit prays for us with groanings that cannot be expressed in words. ²⁷ And the Father who knows all hearts knows what the Spirit is saying, for the Spirit pleads for us believers in harmony with God's own will.

²⁸ And we know that God causes everything to work together for the good of those who love God and are called according to his purpose for them. ²⁹ For God knew his people in advance, and he chose them to become like his Son, so that his Son would be the firstborn among many brothers and sisters. ³⁰ And having chosen them, he called them to come to him. And having called them, he gave them right standing with himself. And having given them right standing, he gave them his glory.

Nothing Can Separate Us from God's Love

 Romans 8:31
Another way to read this verse is instead of the word "if", use the word "because". We often forget that God is on our side. And *because* God is for us, does it matter who is against us? In the end, those people really aren't choosing against us, they are choosing against God.

³¹ What shall we say about such wonderful things as these? If God is for us, who can ever be against us? ³² Since he did not spare even his own Son but gave him up for us all, won't he also give us everything else? ³³ Who dares accuse us whom God has chosen for his own? No one—for God himself has given us right standing with himself.

³⁴ Who then will condemn us? No one—for Christ Jesus died for us and was raised to life for us, and he is sitting in the place of honor at God's right hand, pleading for us.

³⁵ Can anything ever separate us from Christ's love? Does it mean he no longer loves us if we have trouble or calamity, or are persecuted, or hungry, or destitute, or in danger, or threatened with death?

Romans 8:38-39 If you have ever asked the question "am I really saved or do I need to do this again?". Once saved, always saved is the opposite to that argument. This verse supports the "once saved, always saved". If you have taken the step of asking God into your heart, and there was truly a heart change, you can trust that you are a child of God and that he is your Heavenly Father. As his child, nothing – not one single thing or any total number of things combined – could separate us from the love of an all-powerful God.

[36] (As the Scriptures say, "For your sake we are killed every day; we are being slaughtered like sheep.") [37] No, despite all these things, overwhelming victory is ours through Christ, who loved us.

[38] And I am convinced that nothing can ever separate us from God's love. Neither death nor life, neither angels nor demons, neither our fears for today nor our worries about tomorrow—not even the powers of hell can separate us from God's love. [39] No power in the sky above or in the earth below—indeed, nothing in all creation will ever be able to separate us from the love of God that is revealed in

Christ Jesus our Lord.

Introduction to Romans - Chapter 9

There is a turn that takes place in this chapter. Remember that Paul is a Jew and a Roman citizen. He knows that the Jews have been looking for the Messiah for the last 400 years. They are looking for the Messiah to come and save them against the powerful Romans.

Paul's frustration is that most of the Jews didn't believe in Jesus as the Messiah. Remember that Paul had a personal meeting with the risen Jesus. The Jews did not have this. Many of the Jews did not believe that Jesus was the Messiah they had been looking for all this time.

Paul shares with the Romans, as he does with readers in this chapter, examples from the Old Testament of when Israel rejected God and his message. This was happening at the time Paul wrote this letter just as it is today.

Romans 9:2-3 How much did Paul love "his people", which he calls his brothers and sisters? He was willing to sacrifice his life for them just as Jesus did for us. He was willing to do this so that they might be saved. This is a struggle for many of us because we cannot imagine sacrificing our money, time, lifestyle, riches, energy, etc. let alone our entire life so that someone might take a step of faith toward God.

Romans Chapter Nine

God's Selection of Israel

[1] With Christ as my witness, I speak with utter truthfulness. My conscience and the Holy Spirit confirm it. [2] My heart is filled with bitter sorrow and unending grief [3] for my people, my Jewish brothers and sisters. I would be willing to be forever cursed—cut off from Christ!—if that would save them. [4] They are the people of Israel, chosen to be God's adopted children. God revealed his glory to them. He made covenants with them and gave them his law. He gave them the privilege of worshiping him and receiving his wonderful promises. [5] Abraham, Isaac, and Jacob are their ancestors, and Christ himself was an Israelite as far as his human nature is concerned. And he is God, the one who rules over everything and is worthy of eternal praise! Amen.

⁶ Well then, has God failed to fulfill his promise to Israel? No, for not all who are born into the nation of Israel are truly members of God's people! ⁷ Being descendants of Abraham doesn't make them truly Abraham's children. For the Scriptures say, "Isaac is the son through whom your descendants will be counted," though Abraham had other children, too. ⁸ This means that Abraham's physical descendants are not necessarily children of God. Only the children of the promise are considered to be Abraham's children. ⁹ For God had promised, "I will return about this time next year, and Sarah will have a son."

¹⁰ This son was our ancestor Isaac. When he married Rebekah, she gave birth to twins. ¹¹ But before they were born, before they had done anything good or bad, she received a message from God. (This message shows that God chooses people according to his own purposes;

Romans 9:6 Many times there are words in the Bible we read but don't consider what they mean. Israel is a perfect example of this. Israel means "governed by God". In this verse, Paul is sharing that there were some who were governed by God that weren't even believers!

Romans 9:17-18
There were 20 times where Pharaoh's heart was hardened. 10 times God hardened his heart while the other 10 times Pharaoh did it on his own. The amazing part was that Pharaoh got to witness all of God's miracles. But, because of his past and his role, he believed that he, too, was a god, even though he couldn't perform miracles on his own. Even after witnessing all the amazing miracles, Pharaoh still put himself above God. You can read about Pharaoh in the book of Exodus in the Old Testament.

[12] he calls people, but not according to their good or bad works.) She was told, "Your older son will serve your younger son." [13] In the words of the Scriptures, "I loved Jacob, but I rejected Esau."

[14] Are we saying, then, that God was unfair? Of course not! [15] For God said to Moses,

"I will show mercy to anyone I choose,
and I will show compassion to anyone I choose."

[16] So it is God who decides to show mercy. We can neither choose it nor work for it.

[17] For the Scriptures say that God told Pharaoh, "I have appointed you for the very purpose of displaying my power in you and to spread my fame throughout the earth." [18] So you see, God chooses to show mercy to some, and he chooses to harden the hearts of others so they refuse to listen.

¹⁹ Well then, you might say, "Why does God blame people for not responding? Haven't they simply done what he makes them do?"

²⁰ No, don't say that. Who are you, a mere human being, to argue with God? Should the thing that was created say to the one who created it, "Why have you made me like this?" ²¹ When a potter makes jars out of clay, doesn't he have a right to use the same lump of clay to make one jar for decoration and another to throw garbage into?

²² In the same way, even though God has the right to show his anger and his power, he is very patient with those on whom his anger falls, who are destined for destruction. ²³ He does this to make the riches of his glory shine even brighter on those to whom he shows mercy, who were prepared in advance for glory. ²⁴ And we are among those whom he selected, both from the Jews and from the Gentiles.

Romans 9:20-21 Paul wrote in another book of the Bible that we are all members of one body. We all have a role in being a part of that body. Our human nature, however, wants to push back against God because of this. As Paul shares in verse 21, God can do anything with us and use us in any way because we are all moldable. What he makes us into is his choice - that is God being God. It is our choice whether to be shaped and used by God for others to see.

<thumbnail> **Romans 9:25-29**

One of the goals of the Emoji Bible Project is pointing you to the Bible. Each of the books of the project makes up a book or small portion of the Bible. In these verses Paul is quoting from Old Testament scriptures. You can read Romans 9:25 in Hosea 2:23. You can read Romans 9:26 in Hosea 1:10. You can read Romans 9:27-28 in Isaiah 10: 22-23. And you can read Romans 9:29 in Isaiah 1:9. What a great challenge to find a Bible you understand (that is why we chose the New Living Translation version of the Bible) and to read these verses for yourself. Remember, when you use the Bible as a whole, you will find these verses Paul quotes in Romans in the Old Testament!

[25] Concerning the Gentiles, God says in the prophecy of Hosea,

"Those who were not my people,
    I will now call my people.
    And I will love those
    whom I did not love before."

[26] And,

"Then, at the place where they were told,
        'You are not my people,'
    there they will be called
    'children of the living God.'"

[27] And concerning Israel, Isaiah the prophet cried out,

"Though the people of Israel are as numerous as the sand of the seashore,
    only a remnant will be saved.

[28] For the Lord will carry out his sentence upon the earth
    quickly and with finality."

²⁹ And Isaiah said the same thing in another place:

"If the Lord of Heaven's Armies
    had not spared a few of our
    children,
we would have been wiped out
    like Sodom,
        destroyed like Gomorrah."

Israel's Unbelief

³⁰ What does all this mean? Even though the Gentiles were not trying to follow God's standards, they were made right with God. And it was by faith that this took place. ³¹ But the people of Israel, who tried so hard to get right with God by keeping the law, never succeeded. ³² Why not? Because they were trying to get right with God by keeping the law instead of by trusting in him. They stumbled over the great rock in their path. ³³ God warned them of this in the Scriptures when he said,

"I am placing a stone in Jerusalem
    that makes people stumble,
        a rock that makes them fall.
But anyone who trusts in him
    will never be disgraced."

Romans 9:30 This is another verse that shares with us that we cannot earn our way into heaven. Remember that there are two kinds of people in the Bible: the Jews and the Gentiles. A Jew is anyone that is from Jerusalem, or, as a whole country or region, Israel. Anyone that is not a Jew is a Gentile. Most of us are Gentiles. To be made right with God isn't achieved by how good we are or by what we do. As this verse shares it is by faith.

Introduction to Romans - Chapter 10

Paul has a desire for everyone to know who Jesus is.

This includes the Jews, who had been waiting for the Messiah for so long, but they were missing him, yet he was right there with them in the person of Jesus.

The Jews had become so focused on their observance of the commands in the Torah, that they did not see what was right in front of them.

The Torah is the first five books of the Old Testament in what is our Bible today. Jews used this as the basis for their relationship with God. The Jews did not recognize what God was doing for them through Jesus.

Romans 10:1 Paul knew the law and understood God's love for everyone. This included the Jews who were from Israel and known throughout the Bible as God's chosen people. Paul wanted everybody to be saved and to spend eternity with a loving savior in Jesus, regardless of race, gender, or religion. This is something that we should have a heart for and commit to prayer, just as Paul did here, as well.

¹ Dear brothers and sisters, the longing of my heart and my prayer to God is for the people of Israel to be saved. ² I know what enthusiasm they have for God, but it is misdirected zeal. ³ For they don't understand God's way of making people right with himself. Refusing to accept God's way, they cling to their own way of getting right with God by trying to keep the law. ⁴ For Christ has already accomplished the purpose for which the law was given. As a result, all who believe in him are made right with God.

Salvation Is for Everyone

⁵ For Moses writes that the law's way of making a person right with God requires obedience to all of its commands. ⁶ But faith's way of getting right with God says, "Don't say in your heart, 'Who will go up to heaven?' (to bring Christ down to earth). ⁷ And don't say, 'Who will go down to the place of the dead?' (to bring Christ back to life again)."

[8] In fact, it says,

> "The message is very close at
> hand;
>   it is on your lips and in your
> heart."

And that message is the very
message about faith that we
preach:

[9] If you openly declare that Jesus is
Lord and believe in your heart that
God raised him from the dead,
you will be saved. [10] For it is by
believing in your heart that you are
made right with God, and it is by
openly declaring your faith that
you are saved. [11] As the Scriptures
tell us, "Anyone who trusts in him
will never be disgraced." [12] Jew and
Gentile are the same in this
respect. They have the same Lord,
who gives generously to all who
call on him. [13] For "Everyone who
calls on the name of

the LORD will be saved."

 **Romans 10:9-10**
This is the fourth set of
verses of the "Roman
Road", which teaches us
how to share salvation with
someone that wants to
know for sure they have a
place in Heaven with a
loving Heavenly Father.

This is a deep personal
choice that each of us make
when it comes to our
relationship with God. This
is where we take a step of
faith and admit that we
need to be saved. This is
also where we put our trust
in Jesus to be our personal
savior.

*(Here are the verses you
can follow, in order, in the
book of Romans for the
plan of salvation: Romans
3:23; Romans 5:8; Romans
6:23; Romans 8:1; Romans
10:8-13.)*

Romans 10:15 As a believer, our walk of faith starts as a disciple. A disciple is someone who learns and walks alongside of others as they grow in their faith. Eventually, a transition has to take place from disciple to apostle. An apostle is someone who carries the message to share with others. They become a messenger, or a missionary, just as the Apostle Paul was.

¹⁴ But how can they call on him to save them unless they believe in him? And how can they believe in him if they have never heard about him? And how can they hear about him unless someone tells them? ¹⁵ And how will anyone go and tell them without being sent? That is why the Scriptures say, "How beautiful are the feet of messengers who bring good news!"

¹⁶ But not everyone welcomes the Good News, for Isaiah the prophet said, "LORD, who has believed our message?" ¹⁷ So faith comes from hearing, that is, hearing the Good News about Christ. ¹⁸ But I ask, have the people of Israel actually heard the message? Yes, they have:

"The message has gone throughout
the earth,
and the words to all the
world."

¹⁹ But I ask, did the people of Israel really understand? Yes, they did, for even in the time of Moses, God said,

"I will rouse your jealousy through people who are not even a nation.
    I will provoke your anger through the foolish Gentiles."

20 And later Isaiah spoke boldly for God, saying,

"I was found by people who were not looking for me.
    I showed myself to those who were not asking for me."

21 But regarding Israel, God said,

"All day long I opened my arms to them,
    but they were disobedient
    and rebellious."

Romans 10:20-21 At the beginning of chapter 10 we shared the Gospel is for both the Jew and the Gentile. (See study note on Romans 10:1) God's love is for everyone. This verse shows the person that will miss God not only in this lifetime but for eternity. It doesn't matter who it is – if it is a Jew or a Gentile. The one who will miss God doesn't want to obey and is rebellious. That person will miss out on the love of God both now and forever.

Introduction to Romans - Chapter 11

God hasn't given up on the Jewish people. But God sent his son Jesus so that all might be saved. His invitation to know him personally was to everyone, both Jew and Gentile. Not once did God say that didn't include the Gentiles. For the Jew, though, that also meant that God's love also included the Gentile. This was difficult for the Jews to understand, as they had been taught their whole lives that they were God's chosen people.

Romans 11:1 This verse shares with us that there are Jews who also believe that Jesus is the Messiah, the son of God. Remember that Paul was a Jew. Remember, too, that all of Jesus's disciples were Jews. Lastly, remember that the first missionaries who went out to share the Good News would also have been Jews. All those people became believers when they trusted that God had sent his one and only son to die for each of them. And, when Jesus rose from the dead to show them they could have eternal life, each of them believed.

Romans Chapter Eleven

God's Mercy on Israel

[1] I ask, then, has God rejected his own people, the nation of Israel? Of course not! I myself am an Israelite, a descendant of Abraham and a member of the tribe of Benjamin.

[2] No, God has not rejected his own people, whom he chose from the very beginning. Do you realize what the Scriptures say about this? Elijah the prophet complained to God about the people of Israel and said, [3] "Lord, they have killed your prophets and torn down your altars. I am the only one left, and now they are trying to kill me, too."

[4] And do you remember God's reply? He said, "No, I have 7,000 others who have never bowed down to Baal!"

⁵ It is the same today, for a few of the people of Israel have remained faithful because of God's grace—his undeserved kindness in choosing them. ⁶ And since it is through God's kindness, then it is not by their good works. For in that case, God's grace would not be what it really is—free and undeserved.

⁷ So this is the situation: Most of the people of Israel have not found the favor of God they are looking for so earnestly. A few have—the ones God has chosen—but the hearts of the rest were hardened. ⁸ As the Scriptures say,

> "God has put them into a deep sleep.
> To this day he has shut their eyes
> so they do not see,
>   and closed their ears so they
>   do not hear."

⁹ Likewise, David said,

> "Let their bountiful table become a snare,
>   a trap that makes them think all is well.

Romans 11:7 The Jews at this time saw the miracles that Jesus did. They also saw him die on the cross and come back from the dead. Somehow, they chose not to believe. The very Messiah they were looking for was with them, yet they could not see Jesus for who he was. It came to a point then, just as it comes to a point now, that they hardened their hearts to the point they wouldn't believe. This doesn't just happen to the Jews. It can happen to us, as well. As this verse points out, that is what most people will choose.

Romans 11:12

Jesus's promise to all that believe goes beyond eternal life. It starts in this life. He promised us a counselor and a comforter through his Holy Spirit when he left this world (John 14:26). The Holy Spirit brings us peace and hope to any of us that believe. How much different would this world be if people walked as if they knew they had the promise of peace and hope of eternity in their lives? How much different would your world look if you walked in it holding on to that same promise?

Let their blessings cause them to stumble,
and let them get what they deserve.
[10] Let their eyes go blind so they cannot see,
and let their backs be bent forever."

[11] Did God's people stumble and fall beyond recovery? Of course not! They were disobedient, so God made salvation available to the Gentiles. But he wanted his own people to become jealous and claim it for themselves. [12] Now if the Gentiles were enriched because the people of Israel turned down God's offer of salvation, think how much greater a blessing the world will share when they finally accept it.

[13] I am saying all this especially for you Gentiles. God has appointed me as the apostle to the Gentiles. I stress this,

¹⁴ for I want somehow to make the people of Israel jealous of what you Gentiles have, so I might save some of them. ¹⁵ For since their rejection meant that God offered salvation to the rest of the world, their acceptance will be even more wonderful. It will be life for those who were dead! ¹⁶ And since Abraham and the other patriarchs were holy, their descendants will also be holy—just as the entire batch of dough is holy because the portion given as an offering is holy. For if the roots of the tree are holy, the branches will be, too.

¹⁷ But some of these branches from Abraham's tree—some of the people of Israel—have been broken off. And you Gentiles, who were branches from a wild olive tree, have been grafted in. So now you also receive the blessing God has promised Abraham and his children, sharing in the rich nourishment from the root of God's special olive tree.

Romans 11:17 When a tree stops producing fruit, the old branches that stopped making the fruit were cut off as they were no longer useful. A branch was cut off a younger tree and inserted into where the old branch was growing. Eventually this new branch started to grow fruit, as it was fed from the old tree base and had now become part of the tree.

Romans 11:19-21

These verses point to the fact that it isn't enough to just believe. James tells us that even the demons believe. Is there a difference in your life that shows that you believe in a loving God? You will see this written many times in this project, as it is such an important reminder: it isn't faith or works, it isn't faith and works, it is faith that works. Is their evidence of your faith in God by the way you speak, treat, and love others? Does it reflect a loving God? If there isn't...well, just read these verses again out loud and Paul will share why it is so important to live what you believe every day.

¹⁸ But you must not brag about being grafted in to replace the branches that were broken off. You are just a branch, not the root.

¹⁹ "Well," you may say, "those branches were broken off to make room for me." ²⁰ Yes, but remember—those branches were broken off because they didn't believe in Christ, and you are there because you do believe. So don't think highly of yourself, but fear what could happen. ²¹ For if God did not spare the original branches,

he won't spare you either.

²² Notice how God is both kind and severe. He is severe toward those who disobeyed, but kind to you if you continue to trust in his kindness. But if you stop trusting, you also will be cut off. ²³ And if the people of Israel turn from their unbelief, they will be grafted in again, for God has the power to graft them back into the tree.

²⁴ You, by nature, were a branch cut from a wild olive tree. So if God was willing to do something contrary to nature by grafting you into his cultivated tree, he will be far more eager to graft the original branches back into the tree where they belong.

God's Mercy Is for Everyone

²⁵ I want you to understand this mystery, dear brothers and sisters, so that you will not feel proud about yourselves. Some of the people of Israel have hard hearts, but this will last only until the full number of Gentiles comes to Christic. ²⁶ And so all Israel will be saved. As the Scriptures say,

"The one who rescues will come from Jerusalem,
and he will turn Israel away from ungodliness.
²⁷ And this is my covenant with them,
that I will take away their sins."

²⁸ Many of the people of Israel are now enemies of the Good News, and this benefits you Gentiles.

Romans 11:25 You will hear people talk about the "end times" and "Jesus is coming back" as this points to the book of Revelation and is the final step every believer is waiting to have happen. Jesus said in Mark 13:32 that none of us know when that time is coming. Paul gives us one answer to this mystery when he shares it will happen when the full number of Gentiles comes to know Jesus as their savior. Only God knows when that will happen, but, when it does, that's it!

Romans 11:28

Abraham was known as the father of all nations. Isaac was the son born to him and Sarah in his old age. Abraham was 100 years old when Isaac was born (Genesis 21:5)! Jacob was the second of a set of twins born to Isaac. You can read their stories in the book of Genesis, the very first book of the Bible.

Yet they are still the people he loves because he chose their ancestors Abraham, Isaac, and Jacob.

²⁹ For God's gifts and his call can never be withdrawn. ³⁰ Once, you Gentiles were rebels against God, but when the people of Israel rebelled against him, God was merciful to you instead. ³¹ Now they are the rebels, and God's mercy has come to you so that they, too, will share in God's mercy. ³² For God has imprisoned everyone in disobedience so he could have mercy on everyone.

³³ Oh, how great are God's riches and wisdom and knowledge! How impossible it is for us to understand his decisions and his ways!

³⁴ For who can know the LORD's thoughts?
Who knows enough to give him advice?
³⁵ And who has given him so much that he needs to pay it back?

[36] For everything comes from him and exists by his power and is intended for his glory. All glory to him forever! Amen.

Introduction to Romans - Chapter 12

This is a very personal chapter about the role of the believer. It starts with a discussion about God's will for each of us. In this chapter, Paul explores what unity looks like. He shares that everybody should be using their own unique passions, gifts, and talents to serve each other and look out for one another. We are to be a community of peace and both Jewish and non-Jewish Christians need to learn how to love and forgive each other.

Romans 12:1-2 Each of us falls into one of two categories when it comes to our everyday walk: conformers or transformers. Conformers change based on everything that is going on around them – peoples actions, what they read or hear, and what is happening in the world are examples of these.

Transformers change based on what is going on inside of them. The thoughts we have, the words that come out of our mouths, finding peace, knowing there is hope, and choosing to love others because God loved us first are examples of these. Which of these two are you now? Which of these two do you want to be?

Romans Chapter Twelve

A Living Sacrifice to God

[1] And so, dear brothers and sisters, I plead with you to give your bodies to God because of all he has done for you. Let them be a living and holy sacrifice—the kind he will find acceptable. This is truly the way to worship him. [2] Don't copy the behavior and customs of this world, but let God transform you into a new person by changing the way you think. Then you will learn to know God's will for you, which is good and pleasing and perfect.

[3] Because of the privilege and authority God has given me, I give each of you this warning: Don't think you are better than you really are. Be honest in your evaluation of yourselves, measuring yourselves by the faith God has given us. [4] Just as our bodies have many parts and each part has a special function, [5] so it is with Christ's body. We are many parts of one body, and we all belong to each other.

⁶ In his grace, God has given us different gifts for doing certain things well. So if God has given you the ability to prophesy, speak out with as much faith as God has given you. ⁷ If your gift is serving others, serve them well. If you are a teacher, teach well. ⁸ If your gift is to encourage others, be encouraging. If it is giving, give generously. If God has given you leadership ability, take the responsibility seriously. And if you have a gift for showing kindness to others, do it gladly.

⁹ Don't just pretend to love others. Really love them. Hate what is wrong. Hold tightly to what is good. ¹⁰ Love each other with genuine affection, and take delight in honoring each other. ¹¹ Never be lazy, but work hard and serve the Lord enthusiastically. ¹² Rejoice in our confident hope. Be patient in trouble, and keep on praying. ¹³ When God's people are in need, be ready to help them. Always be eager to practice hospitality.

Romans 12:6-8 God has given each of us a gift or set of gifts. The Bible refers to these as spiritual gifts as they come through the Holy Spirit. For a list of the different kinds of spiritual gifts, read 1 Corinthians chapter 12.

Romans 12:6-8 When we share the gifts that God has given us with others, we should do so to the best of our ability (Read Colossians 3:17). Why? Think of it this way: we are showing God to others when we use the gift(s) he has given us. You may be the only Jesus the person you are sharing your gift with sees that day!

Romans 12:19

When someone does something bad to us or does something wrong to someone we love, our first instinct is to get them back or "make it right". As believers this is NOT our job. Verse 19 shares that God will handle it. It may not be in the timeframe we want it to happen, but God will handle it in his way and in his time. Read 1 Peter 5:6 and Galatians 6:9 any time you need encouraged or a reminder of this promise from God!

¹⁴ Bless those who persecute you. Don't curse them; pray that God will bless them. ¹⁵ Be happy with those who are happy, and weep with those who weep. ¹⁶ Live in harmony with each other. Don't be too proud to enjoy the company of ordinary people. And don't think you know it all!

¹⁷ Never pay back evil with more evil. Do things in such a way that everyone can see you are honorable. ¹⁸ Do all that you can to live in peace with everyone.

¹⁹ Dear friends, never take revenge. Leave that to the righteous anger of God. For the Scriptures say,

"I will take revenge;
    I will pay them back,"

says the LORD.

²⁰ Instead,

"If your enemies are hungry, feed them.
If they are thirsty, give them something to drink.
In doing this, you will heap burning coals of shame on their heads."

²¹ Don't let evil conquer you, but conquer evil by doing good.

Romans 12:21 What is "good"? The Bible tells us God is good (Mark 10:18, Luke 18:19). An often repeated saying by believers is that "God is good all the time and all the time God is good". So, how do we do "good"? You do the things that God would do. Jesus said it best when he said to love others as he loved others (Read John 13:34, John 15:12). In the process of doing this, you not only love other people as Jesus did, but you conquer evil, too!

Introduction to Romans - Chapter 13

As a Christian, our focus should be to love God and to love others as ourselves. This kind of love would fulfill the law. To the Jews, this would mean fulfilling all the commands of the Torah.

This is the same love that Jesus showed others. Jesus did this to everyone he came in contact with every day. This chapter focuses on how we should treat people in our schools, where we live, and where we work – in every area of our society.

Romans 13:1 It is not our place to argue with who is in a political office. They have been elected to be there. Understand that we need people in these positions, but that they may or may not reflect God. Either way, we are to submit to elected officials unless it is against God's Word to do so. Remember, God is large and in charge. He has the final say. That person (or people) is only in office for a short term. Our focus shouldn't be on what is temporary, but on what is eternal.

Romans Chapter Thirteen

Respect for Authority

[1] Everyone must submit to governing authorities. For all authority comes from God, and those in positions of authority have been placed there by God. [2] So anyone who rebels against authority is rebelling against what God has instituted, and they will be punished. [3] For the authorities do not strike fear in people who are doing right, but in those who are doing wrong. Would you like to live without fear of the authorities? Do what is right, and they will honor you. [4] The authorities are God's servants, sent for your good. But if you are doing wrong, of course you should be afraid, for they have the power to punish you. They are God's servants, sent for the very purpose of punishing those who do what is wrong. [5] So you must submit to them, not only to avoid punishment, but also to keep a clear conscience.

[6] Pay your taxes, too, for these same reasons. For government workers need to be paid. They are serving God in what they do. [7] Give to everyone what you owe them: Pay your taxes and government fees to those who collect them, and give respect and honor to those who are in authority.

Love Fulfills God's Requirements

[8] Owe nothing to anyone—except for your obligation to love one another. If you love your neighbor, you will fulfill the requirements of God's law.

[9] For the commandments say, "You must not commit adultery. You must not murder. You must not steal. You must not covet." These—and other such commandments—are summed up in this one commandment: "Love your neighbor as yourself."

[10] Love does no wrong to others, so love fulfills the requirements of God's law.

Romans 13:8 One debt that we can never pay off is love. God loved us so much he paid everything he had – his one and only son, Jesus. Jesus said to love others as he loved us. We are to pay the love God gave each of us forward by loving others with the love God first gave us. That love never ends which is why we should never stop loving others.

Romans 13:11 The oldest psalm in the Bible is Psalm 90. It was written by Moses. Verse 12 of that psalm tells us to realize that we only have a little time left, so that we may grow in wisdom. In other words, make the most of your time, especially when it comes to your relationship with God.

11 This is all the more urgent, for you know how late it is; time is running out. Wake up, for our salvation is nearer now than when we first believed. 12 The night is almost gone; the day of salvation will soon be here. So remove your dark deeds like dirty clothes, and put on the shining armor of right living. 13 Because we belong to the day, we must live decent lives for all to see. Don't participate in the darkness of wild parties and drunkenness, or in sexual promiscuity and immoral living, or in quarreling and jealousy. 14 Instead, clothe yourself with the presence of the Lord Jesus Christ. And don't let yourself think about ways to indulge your evil desires.

Introduction to Romans - Chapter 14

Paul starts to focus on the divisions in the church and reminds his readers of the disputes between the non-Jewish and Jewish Christians. These disputes are over areas that seem silly

now, such as food laws and the Sabbath Day only laws.

Paul shares that through love, grace, and forgiveness the

separation between people can be filled. This would bring together the church as a family. As a family the church would be unified in Jesus because of God's grace. Because of God's grace, the church needed to learn how to show that same grace to one another, even when they didn't agree over certain issues.

Romans 14:1-3 The first sacrifice made in the Bible was done by God for Adam and Eve. There was no blood shed until sin entered the world. God killed animals to use their skin/fur to cover Adam and Eve. Before this time, with no blood shed, that would mean they were vegetarians. Does that mean we should all be vegetarians? After sin entered the world, God also gave instructions on how to give sacrifices (the book of Leviticus) and which of these could be eaten. Who is right? In the study note for Romans 13:1, it talks about not arguing over things that are temporary. We should focus on eternity. We eat every day, and it is a personal choice. Is a daily argument something that should get in the way of loving others now when it comes to a personal choice they might make that will last forever?

Romans Chapter Fourteen

The Danger of Criticism

[1] Accept other believers who are weak in faith, and don't argue with them about what they think is right or wrong. [2] For instance, one person believes it's all right to eat anything. But another believer with a sensitive conscience will eat only vegetables. [3] Those who feel free to eat anything must not look down on those who don't. And those who don't eat certain foods must not condemn those who do, for God has accepted them. [4] Who are you to condemn someone else's servants? Their own master will judge whether they stand or fall. And with the Lord's help, they will stand and receive his approval.

[5] In the same way, some think one day is more holy than another day, while others think every day is alike. You should each be fully convinced that whichever day you choose is acceptable.

⌣ **6** Those who worship the Lord on a special day do it to honor him. Those who eat any kind of food do so to honor the Lord, since they give thanks to God before eating. And those who refuse to eat certain foods also want to please the Lord and give thanks to God. **7** For we don't live for ourselves or die for ourselves. **8** If we live, it's to honor the Lord. And if we die, it's to honor the Lord. So whether we live or die, we belong to the Lord.

⌣ **9** Christ died and rose again for this very purpose—to be Lord both of the living and of the dead.

10 So why do you condemn another believer? Why do you look down on another believer? Remember, we will all stand before the judgment seat of God. **11** For the Scriptures say,

"'As surely as I live,' says the LORD,
'every knee will bend to me,
        and every tongue will declare allegiance to God.'"

⌣ **Romans 14:7-8** As a Christian, which means "mini-Christ" (See note on Romans 2:21-24) we are not only a believer, each one of us belong to God. The answer isn't "who we are", it is "whose we are". We honor, live, and die for God with our lives because he first honored, lived, and died for us through his son, Jesus.

Romans 14:12-13

God gave each of us twice as many ears (2) as he did a mouth (1). A good way to help us when it comes to complaining, arguing, or, as verse 13 states, condemning (judging) each other is to listen twice as much as we speak. After all, as verse 12 shares, we will all have a discussion with God about this one day.

[12] Yes, each of us will give a personal account to God. [13] So let's stop condemning each other. Decide instead to live in such a way that you will not cause another believer to stumble and fall.

[14] I know and am convinced on the authority of the Lord Jesus that no food, in and of itself, is wrong to eat. But if someone believes it is wrong, then for that person it is wrong. [15] And if another believer is distressed by what you eat, you are not acting in love if you eat it. Don't let your eating ruin someone for whom Christ died. [16] Then you will not be criticized for doing something you believe is good. [17] For the Kingdom of God is not a matter of what we eat or drink, but of living a life of goodness and peace and joy in the Holy Spirit. [18] If you serve Christ with this attitude, you will please God, and others will approve of you, too. [19] So then, let us aim for harmony in the church and try to build each other up.

²⁰ Don't tear apart the work of God over what you eat. Remember, all foods are acceptable, but it is wrong to eat something if it makes another person stumble. ²¹ It is better not to eat meat or drink wine or do anything else if it might cause another believer to stumble. ²² You may believe there's nothing wrong with what you are doing, but keep it between yourself and God. Blessed are those who don't feel guilty for doing something they have decided is right. ²³ But if you have doubts about whether or not you should eat something, you are sinning if you go ahead and do it. For you are not following your convictions. If you do anything you believe is not right, you are

sinning.

Romans 14:20-23 The focus of these verses isn't just about food. It is about doing what is right and what is wrong. In James 4:17 it tells us if we know what we should do and choose not to do it, we are missing God in those moments. When we miss God, the verse in James, just as Romans 14:23 states, means we are sinning.

Introduction to Romans - Chapter 15

It is easy for all of us to get off course. It is easy for us to lose sight of what really matters. It is easy to focus on what is minor and lose focus on the major issue. This was the case in the church at the time Paul wrote the letter to the Romans. It is still a problem today in the modern church. When it comes to our walk of faith as a believer, it means NOT losing focus on the gift that God sent us in the form of his son, Jesus.

Romans 15:1-2

These two verses share that we should be helping each other when it comes to our walk of faith. Too often, we keep to ourselves when it comes to our faith. As a new believer, we need the help of a loving, caring, more experienced believer as we start to grow in our relationship with God. But, as we grow, we should then look to help new believers so they can be strong in their walk of faith, as well. God is a relational God. We need to be relational with others based on our personal relationship with God.

Romans Chapter Fifteen

Living to Please Others

¹We who are strong must be considerate of those who are sensitive about things like this. We must not just please ourselves. ²We should help others do what is right and build them up in the Lord. ³For even Christ didn't live to please himself. As the Scriptures say, "The insults of those who insult you, O God, have fallen on me."⁴ Such things were written in the Scriptures long ago to teach us. And the Scriptures give us hope and encouragement as we wait patiently for God's promises to be fulfilled.

⁵May God, who gives this patience and encouragement, help you live in complete harmony with each other, as is fitting for followers of Christ Jesus.⁶ Then all of you can join together with one voice, giving praise and glory to God, the Father of our Lord Jesus Christ.

⌣ ⁷ Therefore, accept each other just as Christ has accepted you so that God will be given glory.

⌣ ⁸ Remember that Christ came as a servant to the Jews to show that God is true to the promises he made to their ancestors. ⁹ He also came so that the Gentiles might give glory to God for his mercies to them. That is what the psalmist meant when he wrote:

"For this, I will praise you among the Gentiles;
I will sing praises to your name."

¹⁰ And in another place it is written,

"Rejoice with his people, you Gentiles."

¹¹ And yet again,

"Praise the Lord, all you Gentiles.
Praise him, all you people of the earth."

⌣ **Romans 15:6-7** There is something special that takes place when we study God's word together. That is the reason for the Emoji Bible Project. It isn't to be kept to ourselves. It is to be shared with others. God wants everyone to be in heaven. We should want that as well. The only way that is going to happen is if they hear from God. One way they can hear from God is to be in his word. If you are a believer, remember that God has accepted you just the way you are. We need to accept others just as they are, too. It is easy for people to go on their way by themselves. What Paul is sharing here is that we need to be together and have one voice while doing so. Our growth comes when we study God's word. Our relationships with God and others grow when we do this together.

Romans 15:12 This is a verse we read and pass over but it is very important. The verse here is what is known as a fulfillment of prophecy. In other words, it was written in the Old Testament, in this case the book of Isaiah, and came true hundreds and hundreds of years later. Jesus was a relative of King David. You can read about King David in the Old Testament. Their entire family tree can be found in Matthew 1:1-17. These verses will take you from Abraham, the father of all nations, all the way to Jesus and share every father and son combination along the way.

[12] And in another place Isaiah said,

"The heir to David's throne will come,
and he will rule over the Gentiles.
They will place their hope on him."

[13] I pray that God, the source of hope, will fill you completely with joy and peace because you trust in him. Then you will overflow with confident hope through the power of the Holy Spirit.

Paul's Reason for Writing

[14] I am fully convinced, my dear brothers and sisters, that you are full of goodness. You know these things so well you can teach each other all about them. [15] Even so, I have been bold enough to write about some of these points, knowing that all you need is this reminder. For by God's grace,

¹⁶ I am a special messenger from Christ Jesus to you Gentiles. I bring you the Good News so that I might present you as an acceptable offering to God, made holy by the Holy Spirit. ¹⁷ So I have reason to be enthusiastic about all Christ Jesus has done through me in my service to God. ¹⁸ Yet I dare not boast about anything except what Christ has done through me, bringing the Gentiles to God by my message and by the way I worked among them.¹⁹ They were convinced by the power of miraculous signs and wonders and by the power of God's Spirit. In this way, I have fully presented the Good News of Christ from Jerusalem all the way to Illyricum.

²⁰ My ambition has always been to preach the Good News where the name of Christ has never been heard, rather than where a church has already been started by someone else. ²¹ I have been following the plan spoken of in the Scriptures, where it says,

Romans 15:16-17
Here is part of the process that each of us has as a believer. We take a step of faith and accept Jesus as our personal savior. At that point we become a disciple. We grow as a disciple through God's word and around other believers who help us to grow in what we know. The next step is to become an apostle. Paul was known as an apostle because after he was a disciple, he took the message to many different places in the world. He was the special messenger as he started churches in many different areas. It is why we have his letters to the Galatians, Ephesians, Colossians, Thessalonians, and Corinthians (Which you can read in *"EMOJIs and the Missionary Journeys of Paul"*. The Apostle Paul went to others to share the Good News...God's News... which is another term for the Gospel!

"Those who have never been told about him will see,
and those who have never heard of him will understand."

²² In fact, my visit to you has been delayed so long because I have been preaching in these places.

Paul's Travel Plans

²³ But now I have finished my work in these regions, and after all these long years of waiting, I am eager to visit you. ²⁴ I am planning to go to Spain, and when I do, I will stop off in Rome. And after I have enjoyed your fellowship for a little while, you can provide for my journey.

²⁵ But before I come, I must go to Jerusalem to take a gift to the believers there. ²⁶ For you see, the believers in Macedonia and Achaia have eagerly taken up an offering for the poor among the believers in Jerusalem.

²⁷ They were glad to do this because they feel they owe a real debt to them. Since the Gentiles received the spiritual blessings of the Good News from the believers in Jerusalem, they feel the least they can do in return is to help them financially. ²⁸ As soon as I have delivered this money and completed this good deed of theirs, I will come to see you on my way to Spain. ²⁹ And I am sure that when I come, Christ will richly bless our time together.

³⁰ Dear brothers and sisters, I urge you in the name of our Lord Jesus Christ to join in my struggle by praying to God for me. Do this because of your love for me, given to you by the Holy Spirit. ³¹ Pray that I will be rescued from those in Judea who refuse to obey God. Pray also that the believers there will be willing to accept the donation I am taking to Jerusalem. ³² Then, by the will of God, I will be able to come to you with a joyful heart, and we will be an encouragement to each other.

Romans 15:30-31
Here we find Paul asking for prayer. Notice that he is asking other believers to keep him in their prayers. In these verses Paul is very specific about his prayer request. There are times when we need to be specific and other times, especially if it is something very personal, we may not share as much. This is a very important part of our walk. We need to pray for other people. But at times, we also need to ask others to pray for us. When we do this, we are following the example that Paul gives us in these verses.

Romans 15:33 The final verse of this chapter ends with a reminder that God is always ready to give. This verse shares that God gives us his peace, and God is willing to give this to everyone.

[33] And now may God, who gives us his peace, be with you all. Amen.

Introduction to Romans - Chapter 16

This "book" was actually a letter written to the Romans.

Paul didn't write this knowing that it would one day be a part of a book, which we now read as the Bible. When the Bible was translated, it was put into chapter form with verses which were numbered. This final chapter is Paul closing out his letter. This means it is very personal to people that he has in

his life as friends and partners in ministry.

Romans 16:1-2

There are many churches that believe that a deacon should only be a man. A deacon is a servant. They serve the church and the people in it. This verse shows us that this is a role that can be filled by both men and women, as you can see by the example of Phoebe in these verses. Part of being a deacon is to always be willing to help others, just as Phoebe did.

Romans Chapter Sixteen

Paul Greets His Friends

¹ I commend to you our sister Phoebe, who is a deacon in the church in Cenchrea. ² Welcome her in the Lord as one who is worthy of honor among God's people. Help her in whatever she needs, for she has been helpful to many, and especially to me.

³ Give my greetings to Priscilla and Aquila, my co-workers in the ministry of Christ Jesus. ⁴ In fact, they once risked their lives for me. I am thankful to them, and so are all the Gentile churches. ⁵ Also give my greetings to the church that meets in their home.
Greet my dear friend Epenetus. He was the first person from the province of Asia to become a follower of Christ. ⁶ Give my greetings to Mary, who has worked so hard for your benefit. ⁷ Greet Andronicus and Junia, my fellow Jews, who were in prison with me. They are highly respected among the apostles and became followers of Christ before I did.

⁸ Greet Ampliatus, my dear friend in the Lord. ⁹ Greet Urbanus, our co-worker in Christ, and my dear friend Stachys.

¹⁰ Greet Apelles, a good man whom Christ approves. And give my greetings to the believers from the household of Aristobulus. ¹¹ Greet Herodion, my fellow Jew. Greet the Lord's people from the household of Narcissus.¹² Give my greetings to Tryphena and Tryphosa, the Lord's workers, and to dear Persis, who has worked so hard for the Lord. ¹³ Greet Rufus, whom the Lord picked out to be his very own; and also his dear mother, who has been a mother to me.

¹⁴ Give my greetings to Asyncritus, Phlegon, Hermes, Patrobas, Hermas, and the brothers and sisters who meet with them. ¹⁵ Give my greetings to Philologus, Julia, Nereus and his sister, and to Olympas and all the believers who meet with them.

Romans 16:8-15 We read Romans as a book, chapter by chapter. This "book" was written as a letter. In these verses, Paul is starting to say his goodbyes to all his friends before he finishes the letter.

Romans 16:17-18

Paul is ending this letter with a final warning in these verses. It deals with the people we hang out with or have as a part of our lives. There are certain people we just need to stay away from when it comes to our walk of faith. An easy way to know who these people are is this: are they wanting you to do something because it will help you grow as a person? Or are they saying or doing things because it is what is best for them? Paul is warning us to be careful as this can cause division in the church and in your life.

¹⁶ Greet each other with a sacred kiss. All the churches of Christ send you their greetings.

Paul's Final Instructions

¹⁷ And now I make one more appeal, my dear brothers and sisters. Watch out for people who cause divisions and upset people's faith by teaching things contrary to what you have been taught. Stay away from them. ¹⁸ Such people are not serving Christ our Lord; they are serving their own personal interests. By smooth talk and glowing words they deceive innocent people. ¹⁹ But everyone knows that you are obedient to the Lord. This makes me very happy. I want you to be wise in doing right and to stay innocent of any wrong. ²⁰ The God of peace will soon crush Satan under your feet. May the grace of our Lord Jesus be with you.

²¹ Timothy, my fellow worker, sends you his greetings, as do Lucius, Jason, and Sosipater, my fellow Jews.

²² I, Tertius, the one writing this letter for Paul, send my greetings, too, as one of the Lord's followers.

²³ Gaius says hello to you. He is my host and also serves as host to the whole church. Erastus, the city treasurer, sends you his greetings, and so does our brother Quartus.

²⁵ Now all glory to God, who is able to make you strong, just as my Good News says. This message about Jesus Christ has revealed his plan for you Gentiles, a plan kept secret from the beginning of time. ²⁶ But now as the prophets foretold and as the eternal God has commanded, this message is made known to all Gentiles everywhere, so that they too might believe and obey him. ²⁷ All glory to the only wise God, through Jesus Christ, forever. Amen.

Romans 16:22 Here we see that Paul was not actually the person who wrote the letter. It was written by one of the people who was in ministry alongside of him named Tertius. We don't know why Paul had him write for him. The content of the letter to the Romans was from the Apostle Paul. The person who wrote the words was a disciple of his.

Romans 16:25-26 In these final verses, Paul shares a secret about God. His message was never just for the chosen people. It was for everyone. God's message of love is for all of us. For anyone that believes, they can be certain they have a place in heaven. *(Read the study note starting with Romans 3:23 and follow the cross to the very end if you want to understand more about the Good News...and your salvation.)*

Introduction to Micah

Micah is the only prophet in the Old Testament that was sent to both kingdoms of Israel. During this time, the 12 tribes of Israel were fighting each other for many years. This is what is known as a civil war. The 10 tribes from the north and the two tribes from the South were all God's chosen people.

Because the two sides were so focused on fighting each other, they had lost sight of their relationship with God. That meant they stopped talking to God and listening to him. On top of it all, they started worshiping other gods, which was a major reason for all the fighting.

In the end, though, God shows how faithful he is. Things looked terrible for both sides as they had lost their spiritual focus. In each chapter you read you will see how much God loves them. And as they restore their relationship with God, we witness how full of mercy God truly is.

Micah 1:1 In the Old Testament, God shared his message with prophets who then shared that message with the chosen people (the Jewish People or the Israelites). Micah was one of these prophets. He came from the small village of Moresheth and shared God's message with the people in the largest cities of the kingdoms.

Micah 1:1 At this time, Samaria was the capital of the northern kingdom of Israel and Jerusalem was the capital of the southern kingdom of Judah.

Micah Chapter One

¹The Lord gave this message to Micah of Moresheth during the years when Jotham, Ahaz, and Hezekiah were kings of Judah. The visions he saw concerned both Samaria and Jerusalem.

Grief over Samaria and Jerusalem

² Attention! Let all the people of the world listen!
Let the earth and everything in it hear.
The Sovereign Lord is making accusations against you;
the Lord speaks from his holy Temple.
³ Look! The Lord is coming!
He leaves his throne in heaven and tramples the heights of the earth.
⁴ The mountains melt beneath his feet
and flow into the valleys like wax in a fire,
like water pouring down a hill.

⁵ And why is this happening?
   Because of the rebellion of
      Israel—
      yes, the sins of the whole
         nation.
   Who is to blame for Israel's
      rebellion?
   Samaria, its capital city!
Where is the center of idolatry in
      Judah?
   In Jerusalem, its capital!

⁶ "So I, the Lord, will make the
      city of Samaria
      a heap of ruins.
Her streets will be plowed up
      for planting vineyards.
I will roll the stones of her walls
      into the valley below,
      exposing her foundations.

⁷ All her carved images will be
      smashed.
   All her sacred treasures will
      be burned.
These things were bought with the
      money
      earned by her prostitution,
and they will now be carried away
      to pay prostitutes elsewhere."

Micah 1:7 In Exodus 20, God gave the Ten Commandments. The people were putting other gods ahead of God and were making images, like little statues, in these little god's honor. This broke the first two commandments God gave the people. (Read Exodus 20:2-17 for the Ten Commandments.)

Micah 1:8 Every time we see the word "therefore", we should stop and ask, "What is that there for?". In this case we see just how upset Micah was with the people. Mourn means to feel deep sorrow. Lament means a passionate grief or sorrow. Micah was hurting deeply and lovingly because his fellow countrymen and women had turned away from God, and it was difficult to understand why.

[8] Therefore, I will mourn and lament.
I will walk around barefoot and naked.
I will howl like a jackal
and moan like an owl.

[9] For my people's wound
is too deep to heal.
It has reached into Judah,
even to the gates of Jerusalem.

[10] Don't tell our enemies in Gath;
don't weep at all.
You people in Beth-leaphrah,
roll in the dust to show your despair.

[11] You people in Shaphir,
go as captives into exile—naked and ashamed.
The people of Zaanan
dare not come outside their walls.
The people of Beth-ezel mourn,
for their house has no support.

[12] The people of Maroth anxiously wait for relief,
but only bitterness awaits them
as the Lord's judgment reaches
even to the gates of Jerusalem.

¹³ Harness your chariot horses and flee,
you people of Lachish.
You were the first city in Judah
to follow Israel in her rebellion,
and you led Jerusalem into sin.

¹⁴ Send farewell gifts to Moresheth-gath;
there is no hope of saving it.
The town of Aczib
has deceived the kings of Israel.

¹⁵ O people of Mareshah,
I will bring a conqueror to capture your town.
And the leaders of Israel
will go to Adullam.

¹⁶ Oh, people of Judah, shave your heads in sorrow,
for the children you love will be snatched away.
Make yourselves as bald as a vulture,
for your little ones will be exiled to distant lands.

Micah 1:16 It only takes a minute or two to shave all the hair off your head. It takes a long time for it to grow back to where it was before it was cut. Shaving it was a way to show the grief the people had for turning away from God. Growing it back was a daily reminder of how much pain that choice brought them.

Micah 2:2

Remember that money is not evil. The Bible tells us that the *love* of money is evil (1 Timothy 6:10). This is an easy way to remember this verse and the lesson that the Bible teaches: if you invest in people, you will use things. If you invest in things, you will use people. What we invest in and what we use is a personal choice.

Micah Chapter Two

Judgment against Wealthy Oppressors

[1] What sorrow awaits you who lie
awake at night,
thinking up evil plans.
You rise at dawn and hurry to carry
them out,
simply because you have the
power to do so.

[2] When you want a piece of land,
you find a way to seize it.
When you want someone's house,
you take it by fraud and
violence.
You cheat a man of his property,
stealing his family's
inheritance.

[3] But this is what the Lord says:
"I will reward your evil with evil;
you won't be able to pull your
neck out of the noose.
You will no longer walk around
proudly,
for it will be a terrible time."

⁴ In that day your enemies will
make fun of you
by singing this song of despair
about you:
"We are finished,
completely ruined!
God has confiscated our land,
taking it from us.
He has given our fields
to those who betrayed us."

⁵ Others will set your boundaries
then,
and the Lord's people will
have no say
in how the land is divided.

True and False Prophets

⁶ "Don't say such things,"
the people respond.
"Don't prophesy like that.
Such disasters will never
come our way!"

⁷ Should you talk that way, O
family of Israel?
Will the Lord's Spirit have
patience with such behavior?
If you would do what is right,
you would find my words
comforting. 😌

Micah 2:7 Micah is
having a conversation with
the people. He is the
spokesperson for the Lord.
The words he shares here
are words that we can live
by to this day: there is never
a wrong time to do the right
thing. What is the right
thing to do? Follow God's
commands, directions, and
words from the Bible, even
when they hurt a little or
cause us some personal
pain.

[8] Yet to this very hour
my people rise against me like
an enemy!
You steal the shirts right off the
backs
of those who trusted you,
making them as ragged as men
returning from battle.

[9] You have evicted women from
their pleasant homes
and forever stripped their
children of all that God would give
them.

[10] Up! Begone!
This is no longer your land
and home,
for you have filled it with sin
and ruined it completely.

[11] Suppose a prophet full of lies
would say to you,
"I'll preach to you the joys of
wine and alcohol!"
That's just the kind of prophet you

would like!

Hope for Restoration

¹² "Someday, O Israel, I will gather you;
    I will gather the remnant who are left.
I will bring you together again like sheep in a pen,
    like a flock in its pasture.
Yes, your land will again
    be filled with noisy crowds!

¹³ Your leader will break out
    and lead you out of exile,
out through the gates of the enemy cities,
    back to your own land.
Your king will lead you;
    the Lord himself will guide you."

Micah 2:12 Israel had lost its independence for nearly 2000 years as the Jews had been dispersed throughout other cities and countries. In 1948, Israel gained back its name and land to once again be brought back together as a country.

Micah 3:1 The reason the leaders of Israel were supposed to know right from wrong is that they were given the Ten Commandments directly from Moses, who was given these commandments directly from God. God passed them on to Moses who passed them on to the people of Israel. You can read the story of the Ten Commandments in Exodus 20:2-17 or Deuteronomy 5:6-21.

Micah Chapter Three

Judgment against Israel's Leaders

[1] I said, "Listen, you leaders of Israel!
You are supposed to know
right from wrong,
[2] but you are the very ones
who hate good and love evil.
You skin my people alive
and tear the flesh from their bones.
[3] Yes, you eat my people's flesh,
strip off their skin,
and break their bones.
You chop them up
like meat for the cooking pot.
[4] Then you beg the Lord for help
in times of trouble!
Do you really expect him to answer?
After all the evil you have done,
he won't even look at you!"
[5] This is what the Lord says:
"You false prophets are
leading my people astray!
You promise peace for those who give you food,
but you declare war on those
who refuse to feed you.

⁶ Now the night will close around you,
cutting off all your visions.
Darkness will cover you,
putting an end to your predictions.
The sun will set for you prophets,
and your day will come to an end.
⁷ Then you seers will be put to shame,
and you fortune-tellers will be disgraced.
And you will cover your faces
because there is no answer from God."

⁸ But as for me, I am filled with power—
with the Spirit of the Lord.
I am filled with justice and strength
to boldly declare Israel's sin
and rebellion.
⁹ Listen to me, you leaders of Israel!
You hate justice and twist all that is right.
¹⁰ You are building Jerusalem
on a foundation of murder and corruption.

Micah 3:8 In the Old Testament, God spoke through the prophets to get the message to his people. The problem then is the same problem now. They sinned, which means they missed the mark with God, and they rebelled against him, meaning they turned their back on God and did things their own way. Micah wasn't afraid to let the people know that they were sinning as he was just doing what God had given him the power to do in sharing this message.

Micah 3:11 Jesus said in Matthew 6:24 you cannot serve two masters. Jesus went on to say you cannot serve both God and money as you can only be devoted to one. This is a perfect example where the rulers, priests, and prophets were all devoted to money first, leaving God in second place. They had already chosen who they would serve, and it wasn't God, who loved them. It was money, which has no ability to love us back.

¹¹ You rulers make decisions based on bribes;
   you priests teach God's laws only for a price;
you prophets won't prophesy unless you are paid.
   Yet all of you claim to depend on the Lord.
"No harm can come to us," you say, "for the Lord is here among us."

¹² Because of you, Mount Zion will be plowed like an open field;
   Jerusalem will be reduced to ruins!
A thicket will grow on the heights where the Temple now stands.

Micah 4:3 Micah shared that eventually people would turn their weapons, which were meant to take peoples' lives, into tools that could be used to help people live. This would eventually bring peace to people all over the world.

Micah Chapter Four

The Lord's Future Reign

¹ In the last days, the mountain of
the Lord's house
will be the highest of all—
the most important place on
earth.
It will be raised above the other
hills,
and people from all over the
world will stream there to worship.
² People from many nations will
come and say,
"Come, let us go up to the
mountain of the Lord,
to the house of Jacob's God.
There he will teach us his ways,
and we will walk in his paths."
For the Lord's teaching will go out
from Zion;
his word will go out from
Jerusalem.
³ The Lord will mediate between
peoples
and will settle disputes between
strong nations far away.
They will hammer their swords into
plowshares
and their spears into pruning

hooks.

Nation will no longer fight against
nation,
nor train for war anymore.
⁴ Everyone will live in peace and
prosperity,
enjoying their own grapevines
and fig trees,
for there will be nothing to
fear.
The Lord of Heaven's Armies
has made this promise!
⁵ Though the nations around us
follow their idols,
we will follow the Lord our

God forever and ever.

Israel's Return from Exile

⁶ "In that coming day," says
the Lord,
"I will gather together those who
are lame,
those who have been exiles,
and those whom I have filled
with grief.
⁷ Those who are weak will survive
as a remnant;
those who were exiles will
become a strong nation.
Then I, the Lord, will rule from
Jerusalem
as their king forever."

Micah 4:5 This verse also points to the Ten Commandments (Read note on Micah 1:7) where God said not to make any images or follow someone instead of God. That is what idols are. You can look up to people, admire them, be proud of who they are and what they believe, but we can never put them ahead of God. The people we admire are just like you and me and will only last a short time. God will last forever, which is why he is first above everyone and everything.

Micah 4:10 This is a message repeated throughout the Bible and one each of us can hold on to in times of trouble. The Lord not only has the power and ability to rescue us in times of trouble but is also willing to free us from those struggles!

⁸ As for you, Jerusalem,
the citadel of God's people,
your royal might and power
will come back to you again.
The kingship will be restored
to my precious Jerusalem.

⁹ But why are you now screaming in terror?
Have you no king to lead you?
Have your wise people all died?
Pain has gripped you like a woman in childbirth.

¹⁰ Writhe and groan like a woman in labor,
you people of Jerusalem,
for now you must leave this city
to live in the open country.
You will soon be sent in exile
to distant Babylon.
But the Lord will rescue you there;
he will redeem you from the
grip of your enemies.

¹¹ Now many nations have gathered against you.
"Let her be desecrated," they say.
"Let us see the destruction of Jerusalem."

¹² But they do not know the Lord's thoughts

or understand his plan.
These nations don't know
that he is gathering them together
to be beaten and trampled
like sheaves of grain on a threshing floor.
¹³ "Rise up and crush the nations, O Jerusalem!"
says the Lord.
"For I will give you iron horns and bronze hooves,
so you can trample many nations to pieces.
You will present their stolen riches to the Lord,
their wealth to the Lord of all the earth."

Micah 4:12 There is an old saying that goes "if you fail to plan, you plan to fail". There is nothing wrong with us having plans, but, in the end, it is up to us to remember what is shared in Jeremiah 29:11: "I know the plans I have for you. They are plans of good and not disaster, to give you a future and a hope." Despite all the areas we struggle and miss God in our lives at times, he offers us hope through his plan in our lives. We may not know what our future holds, but we know who holds our future!

Micah 5:1-2 There were many villages named Bethlehem in the region, but this one has a very specific name. "Ephrathah" means fruitful. The fruit that would come from this village, according to the verses, was the Ruler. This was the exact village that Jesus would be born.

Micah Chapter Five

[1] Mobilize! Marshal your troops!
The enemy is laying siege to
Jerusalem.
They will strike Israel's leader
in the face with a rod.

A Ruler from Bethlehem

[2] But you, O Bethlehem Ephrathah,
are only a small village among

all the people of Judah.
Yet a ruler of Israel,
whose origins are in the distant
past,
will come from you on my
behalf.
[3] The people of Israel will be
abandoned to their enemies
until the woman in labor gives
birth.
Then at last his fellow countrymen
will return from exile to their
own land.
[4] And he will stand to lead his flock
with the Lord's strength,
in the majesty of the name of
the Lord his God.
Then his people will live there
undisturbed,
for he will be highly honored
around the world.

[5] And he will be the source of
peace.
When the Assyrians invade our
land
and break through our
defenses,
we will appoint seven rulers to
watch over us,
eight princes to lead us.
[6] They will rule Assyria with drawn
swords
and enter the gates of the
land of Nimrod.
He will rescue us from the
Assyrians
when they pour over the
borders to invade our land.

The Remnant Purified

[7] Then the remnant left in Israel
will take their place among
the nations.
They will be like dew sent by
the Lord
or like rain falling on the
grass,
which no one can hold back
and no one can restrain.

Micah 5:15 The problem then is the same problem now and will continue to be a problem for some time. People are always searching and looking for ways to fill their lives away from God. At some point and time, God will have his fill of this, and will show his power for all to see.

8 The remnant left in Israel
will take their place among the nations.
They will be like a lion among the animals of the forest,
like a strong young lion among flocks of sheep and goats,
pouncing and tearing as they go with no rescuer in sight.
9 The people of Israel will stand up to their foes,
and all their enemies will be wiped out.

10 "In that day," says the Lord,
"I will slaughter your horses and destroy your chariots.
11 I will tear down your walls and demolish your defenses.
12 I will put an end to all witchcraft, and there will be no more fortune-tellers.
13 I will destroy all your idols and sacred pillars,
so you will never again worship the work of your own hands.
14 I will abolish your idol shrines with their Asherah poles
and destroy your pagan cities.
15 I will pour out my vengeance on all the nations that refuse to

obey me."

Micah 6:3 This was something we see repeated throughout the Old Testament. The chosen people went their own way without God. They would get in trouble. God would come and rescue them. God finally asks them a question we would all ask, what have I done wrong? God offers us love, peace, and hope. God brings us counsel and guidance in any situation through His word. Why wasn't this enough to these people, then? Why isn't it enough for us, now?

Micah Chapter Six

The Lord's Case against Israel

¹ Listen to what the Lord is saying:
"Stand up and state your case
against me.
Let the mountains and hills be
called to witness your complaints.

² And now, O mountains,
listen to the Lord's complaint!
He has a case against his people.
He will bring charges against
Israel.

³ "O my people, what have I done
to you?
What have I done to make
you tired of me?
Answer me!

⁴ For I brought you out of Egypt
and redeemed you from
slavery.
I sent Moses, Aaron, and
Miriam to help you.

⁵ Don't you remember, my people,
>   how King Balak of Moab
tried to have you cursed
>   and how Balaam son of Beor
blessed you instead?
And remember your journey from
Acacia Grove to Gilgal,
>   when I, the Lord, did
everything I could
>   to teach you about my
faithfulness."

⁶ What can we bring to the Lord?
>   Should we bring him burnt
offerings?
Should we bow before God Most
High
>   with offerings of yearling
calves?

⁷ Should we offer him thousands of
rams
>   and ten thousand rivers of
olive oil?
Should we sacrifice our firstborn
children

>   to pay for our sins?

Micah 6:6-7 Micah's question at this time is the same question he could ask us today. God is always faithful. Always. How can we look so good on the outside and appear so religious, when on the inside we are so far away from God?

Micah 6:9 As you read the book of Micah, you find that God is all powerful and he will not be mocked. This verse shares that if we fear God, we will gain wisdom from that fear. "Fear" here does not mean being afraid. It means to respect. Respecting God for who he is and what he can do in this world and in our lives is a wise move for each of us.

⁸ No, O people, the Lord has told you what is good,
and this is what he requires of you:
to do what is right, to love mercy,
and to walk humbly with your God.

Israel's Guilt and Punishment

⁹ Fear the Lord if you are wise!
His voice calls to everyone in Jerusalem:
"The armies of destruction are coming;
the Lord is sending them.

¹⁰ What shall I say about the homes of the wicked
filled with treasures gained by cheating?
What about the disgusting practice of measuring out grain with dishonest measures?

¹¹ How can I tolerate your merchants
who use dishonest scales and weights?

[12] The rich among you have become wealthy
through extortion and violence.
Your citizens are so used to lying
that their tongues can no longer tell the truth.

[13] "Therefore, I will wound you!
I will bring you to ruin for all your sins.

[14] You will eat but never have enough.
Your hunger pangs and emptiness will remain.
And though you try to save your money,
it will come to nothing in the end.
You will save a little,
but I will give it to those who conquer you.

[15] You will plant crops
but not harvest them.
You will press your olives
but not get enough oil to anoint yourselves.
You will trample the grapes
but get no juice to make your wine.

Micah 6:12 If you read the Ten Commandments (Exodus 20:2-17 or Deuteronomy 5:6-21) you will see a commandment on not bearing false witness, which means to lie. The people at this time lied so often that whenever they spoke, there was no truth in their words. That is how large a little lie had grown into with their words. Jesus shared with us to choose our words carefully because what we say out loud is what is happening in our hearts. (Read Matthew 12:34; Luke 6:45.)

¹⁶ You keep only the laws of evil
King Omri;
you follow only the example of
wicked King Ahab!
Therefore, I will make an example
of you,
bringing you to complete ruin.
You will be treated with contempt,
mocked by all who see you."

Misery Turned to Hope

Micah 7:2 The truth then is the same truth now. It is so hard to find anyone who is seeking God first in everything they say, do, and live in front of God and others.

¹ How miserable I am!
I feel like the fruit picker after the harvest
who can find nothing to eat.
Not a cluster of grapes or a single early fig
can be found to satisfy my hunger.

² The godly people have all disappeared;
not one honest person is left on the earth.
They are all murderers,
setting traps even for their own

brothers.

³ Both their hands are equally skilled at doing evil!
Officials and judges alike demand bribes.
The people with influence get what they want,
and together they scheme to twist justice.

⁴ Even the best of them is like a
brier;
the most honest is as
dangerous as a hedge of thorns.
But your judgment day is coming
swiftly now.
Your time of punishment is
here, a time of confusion.
⁵ Don't trust anyone—
not your best friend or even
your wife!
⁶ For the son despises his father.
The daughter defies her
mother.
The daughter-in-law defies her
mother-in-law.
Your enemies are right in
your own household!

⁷ As for me, I look to
the Lord for help.
I wait confidently for God to
save me,
and my God will certainly

hear me. 👍
⁸ Do not gloat over me, my
enemies!
For though I fall, I will rise
again.
Though I sit in darkness,
the Lord will be my light.

👍 **Micah 7:7** Circle this verse or underline it. Put stars next to it. No matter what the struggle you are going through now or in the future, you can be confident that God will hear you, and will save you. It may not be how or what you expect, but this is a promise as God will never leave you! (Read Deuteronomy 31:6; Hebrews 13:5.)

Micah 7:9 There is a process that happens in this verse. We first need to admit when and where we have sinned against the Lord. Remember that sin means "to miss the mark". Once we take this step, we can talk to the Lord, meaning God, about all the struggles we have. At some point, God will shine his light on everything happening in our lives and then we will be able to see him working in ways only God can.

⁹ I will be patient as
the Lord punishes me,
for I have sinned against him.
But after that, he will take up my case
and give me justice for all I have suffered from my enemies.
The Lord will bring me into the light,
and I will see his righteousness.

¹⁰ Then my enemies will see that
the Lord is on my side.
They will be ashamed that they taunted me, saying,
"So where is the Lord—
that God of yours?"
With my own eyes I will see their downfall;
they will be trampled like mud in the streets.

¹¹ In that day, Israel, your cities will be rebuilt,
and your borders will be extended.

¹² People from many lands will come and honor you—
from Assyria all the way to the towns of Egypt,

from Egypt all the way to the
Euphrates River,
and from distant seas and
mountains.

[13] But the land will become empty
and desolate
because of the wickedness of
those who live there.

The Lord's Compassion on Israel

[14] O Lord, protect your people
with your shepherd's staff;
lead your flock, your special
possession.
Though they live alone in a thicket
on the heights of Mount
Carmel,
let them graze in the fertile
pastures of Bashan and Gilead
as they did long ago.

[15] "Yes," says the Lord,
"I will do mighty miracles for
you, ☺
like those I did when I rescued
you
from slavery in Egypt."

☺ **Micah 7:15** Someone once said the odds of a miracle are one in a million. Every day there are a million children born all over the world. At one point we were one in a million, meaning we were a miracle! This verse shares that God will do mighty miracles for us. You and I are already living miracles. We get to share that miracle with someone every day because of what God has done for us in our lives!

Micah 7:18 What a beautiful image painted in these closing verses of Micah. God doesn't want to be mad at us. He doesn't want to just be "The Lord". He wants to be the "Lord of our lives". Because of this, he won't stay angry at us forever. God's desire is to show us unlimited, unconditional, unfailing love.

¹⁶ All the nations of the world will stand amazed
at what the Lord will do for you.
They will be embarrassed
at their feeble power.
They will cover their mouths in silent awe,
deaf to everything around them.

¹⁷ Like snakes crawling from their holes,
they will come out to meet the Lord our God.
They will fear him greatly,
trembling in terror at his presence.

¹⁸ Where is another God like you,
who pardons the guilt of the remnant,
overlooking the sins of his special people?
You will not stay angry with your people forever,
because you delight in showing unfailing love.

¹⁹ Once again you will have
compassion on us.
You will trample our sins
under your feet
and throw them into the
depths of the ocean!

²⁰ You will show us your
faithfulness and unfailing love
as you promised to our
ancestors Abraham and Jacob long
ago.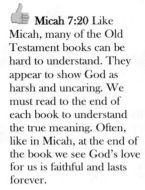

Micah 7:20 Like
Micah, many of the Old
Testament books can be
hard to understand. They
appear to show God as
harsh and uncaring. We
must read to the end of
each book to understand
the true meaning. Often,
like in Micah, at the end of
the book we see God's love
for us is faithful and lasts
forever.

— N🤤TES —

— N🤤TES —

— NOTES —

— N☺TES —

— N😛TES —

— NOTES —

www.PocketFullOfFaith.com

use code EMOJI25 for 25% off any order!